Try to Get Lost

 River Teeth Literary Nonfiction Prize
Daniel Lehman and Joe Mackall, SERIES EDITORS

The River Teeth Literary Nonfiction Prize is awarded to the best work of literary nonfiction submitted to the annual contest sponsored by *River Teeth: A Journal of Nonfiction Narrative.*

Also available in the River Teeth Literary Nonfiction Prize series:

I Am a Stranger Here Myself by Debra Gwartney
MINE: Essays by Sarah Viren
Rough Crossing: An Alaskan Fisherwoman's Memoir by
    Rosemary McGuire
The Girls in My Town: Essays by Angela Morales

Try to Get Lost

Essays on Travel and Place

Joan Frank

University of New Mexico Press | Albuquerque

© 2020 by Joan Frank
All rights reserved. Published 2020
Printed in the United States of America

ISBN 978-0-8263-6137-0 (paper)
ISBN 978-0-8263-6138-7 (e-book)

Library of Congress Cataloging-in-Publication data is on file with the Library
of Congress.

Cover photograph courtesy of Conor Luddy on Unsplash.com
Frontispiece: *Un missionnaire du moyen âge raconte qu'il avait trouvé le
point où le ciel et la Terre se touchent . . . (A medieval missionary tells that
he has found the point where heaven and Earth meet . . .).* Originally printed
in Camille Flammarion, *L'atmosphère: météorologie Populaire* (1888).
Designed by Felicia Cedillos
Composed in Melior LT Std 9.5/14

Andrie, I will find you

What do we do, given life? We move around.

—STEPHEN STILLS AND MANASSAS, "MOVE AROUND"

[Travel] had awakened anxiety in me but even the anxiety, I have to say, was not unwelcome, because I recognized it as the kind of anxiety that would ask to be written about.

—MARTIN AMIS, "OKTOBER," *NEW YORKER*, DEC. 7, 2015

Reasons for joy, whether I live or die, are . . . my constant returns to the country of my heart, my knowledge of it, cognizance through the feet and all the senses, love, love, my love. This is the rallentando before the hurry to the end.

—DAVID CONSTANTINE, "RUE DE LA VIEILLE LANTERNE"

Beautiful my desire, and the place of my desire.

—THEODORE ROETHKE, "THE ROSE"

Contents

Prologue

The Where of It

"We can tell you are from the West," the young man at the art colony told me—his face strangely screwed up, sly, amused—"by the way you take up space in a chair."

We were loitering at the table after dinner. The colony—a famous one situated near the American east coast—was peopled mainly by easterners. I had pushed my chair back from the table and was probably sitting, as I sometimes do, in a sort of yogic twist: one leg folded beneath me, the other crossed over it. After a time I reverse the legs. It soothes my back.

It's not a rude position to look upon—more, I like to think, dancerly.

I live, I should add, near San Francisco.

Though still perhaps only in his twenties, the young man who addressed me had become something of a name, creating a daring series of installations. This notoriety gave his pronunciations a certain clout. Around him at the table that night sat his entourage: male devotees his age, who enjoyed being entertained by his wit.

This happened many years ago. The young man has been dead for some time now, from AIDS-related complications. I can't say I wished him ill, then or later. At the time he administered his cut I was too innocent, too developmentally young as an artist (if not as an ostensibly sophisticated adult) to know how to react, except to be startled. I remember staring at him in blank shock while his minions laughed. Until then—and maybe this is the part I should be ashamed of—I'd never given much thought to the notion of a longstanding rift between east and west, among artists, or anyone.

(History was something I'd memorized to get a grade, then rapidly forgotten.)

I don't know who told the young man where I lived. Maybe I'd told him myself during the back-and-forth of table chat. His remark about the way I sat in a chair was followed by this one: "So what do you think about all day out there? Surfing?"

I was honestly more amazed than offended. Who talked this way? No one, in my experience. Therefore, no precedent could instruct me.

Afterward, in the stew of *l'esprit d'escalier*—the too-late dawning of replies one could or should have made—I concocted what I supposed were little zingers: "And what do *you* think about in your home city? Garbage strikes? Cockroaches? Rent control?"

Unhelpful, even in fantasy.

The above memory leads to another from an earlier time: the dozen years of young adulthood when I lived on a Hawaiian island. I worked for a boho newsweekly whose staff, all transplants from elsewhere, had grown close as family, like a tribe of Lost Boys in Neverland. Our beloved, slightly older editor-founder, wishing to pursue other interests, had hired as his successor a man from a big eastern city who moved to our island for the job. (I'm blurring a few identifying details.)

This gave our ragtag tribe great unease. Who likes change? We wanted Neverland, and our father figure, to stay the same forever. And we feared the noncomprehension of local ways by a newcomer from afar. But we resolved to try to behave like forward-thinking adults. As a welcoming gesture our little band arranged a day trip: we would caravan, in our rusting old cars, along a winding strip of jungly coastal road to a beautiful, remote seaside hamlet. As staff members assembled that morning in the newspaper's parking lot to coordinate cars and passengers, the new editor zoomed up in a shining sports convertible, his young, enviably skinny, edgy girlfriend at his side, both smoking cigarettes like mad.

He leaped from the car, flicked his cigarette to the gravel, and faced us expectantly.

Our new editor was wearing a rose-colored jumpsuit and stylish, lace-up boots. Around his neck he'd flung, Isadora Duncan–style, a very long, silken, fringed scarf.

It was the scarf that undid us all, I think. I've never forgotten it.

We stared. Clearly this man believed himself arrayed for an occasion—his outfit a bold statement, a mark of cool originality and flair.

Please understand that in Hawaii—exempting attorneys heading for court—most people dress in clothing so casual, so faded and softened by time and weather (to the extent that brand name items of Hawaiian "high fashion" are often pre-faded), what people wear becomes almost unperceivable. That's deliberate. In an odd parallel with the most stultified, ingrown old-world village, to live in Hawaii is to understand, by a kind of cultural osmosis, that one presents oneself quietly. Nature accomplishes the flamboyant stuff. The ethos and prevailing attitude among residents there—summing up a great deal—is *easy does it.*

This fellow before us had gotten himself up as though he were about to be filmed in a James Bond sequel.

We Lost Boys and Wendys didn't dare exchange glances. We said nothing. But I'm pretty sure my coworkers and I actually felt sorry for this poor specimen.

Oh, right (we'd have told ourselves silently). He's from the *East.*

Now, consider the fact that you can substitute any place name for *east* and the line will sound equally authoritative, equally sad, equally seasoned. Consider that you can hear that last word, whatever place it describes, uttered with weary scorn.

Oh, right. They're *German. Italian. French. Northern. Asian. Lowlanders.*

American.

Everything is explained in that tone, as our own harbor of superiority feels more snugly fortified.

We can tell you are from *the West.*

This awareness has taken a lifetime to seep in. But over the years I've seen its evidence manifest vastly enough, and repeatedly enough, to cause me to start bringing it up at gatherings.

Here is my late-breaking theory:

Place becomes, finally, the only subject.

Collect any group of people anywhere, for any reason. Artists or farmers, plumbers or housewives, astronauts or gravediggers. Then listen. I guarantee that within minutes their words will make a bee-line to the subject, in one or another form, of place.

Try it. Time it. Whatever the occasion—cocktail party, laundromat, standing in line at the market, bank, zoo. Soon the words veer like iron filings toward the ultimate magnet: *where.* Where we came from, where we are going—five minutes from now or fifty years ago—and everything in between.

So much fills that in-between. The merits, the drawbacks. Report, speculation, opinion. Competitions, parallels. Dreams.

Nightmares. Damnation by definition.

"You don't understand the English," my husband's late mother (a Blackburn, Lancashire native) once declared to me slowly, seated across the room, arms folded, eyes lit with finality, precise weight given to each word. "And you don't—understand—*me.*"

Town versus city. Tame against wild. Arctic, tropic. Mountains, beach. Urban, suburban. Sections, hoods. Backroads, alleyways. Preserves, parks. Latitude, longitude. Goods and services, or their lacks. Beauty or not. Ethnicity or not. Past conditions, future prospects.

Weather! Oh, weather. A concern so at-the-marrow of place, so primal it may have dominated conversation since we could grunt.

"I've always liked Sixth Avenue," I heard a young man say with calm pride to his friend, as the crowd waited for the light to change on a Manhattan corner. As though he had willed the street into being and now felt modestly pleased by its continued success. We like to claim propriety. Live there long enough, you partly own it—even, somehow, partly *created* it.

When we find a place we love, we're torn. Tell everyone—or no one?

Where should we be? Why?

We cannot chop the issue finely enough. We cannot plunge deeply enough. Most interestingly, we can never completely satisfy ourselves in the claims we make for a place, or the questions we raise about it. We chew over the challenge of persuading others, which may be one method of persuading ourselves. We talk to ourselves, troubled, driven, conflicted. Place is obsession, raison d'être, riddle. Expressed most gently it shapes ideas and behaviors, often trying to work itself out through art. (Lowry's Mexico, Bishop's Brazil, O'Keeffe's Southwest.) Expressed most violently it starts (and perpetuates) wars.

We expand, defend, bolster it. Or the reverse: This property is condemned.

An industry is made of Lament for the Lost Place, in every form. Most baffling is the built-in unanswerability to the passionate *cri de coeur* deploring the disintegration, degradation, overpopulation, pollution, hyperinflation of one and another place. The Paris, Rome, New York, the San Francisco or Los Angeles or Honolulu, the shambling Main Street, the old hotel, the original delicatessen or saloon or bookshop, the postcard-exquisite meadow, the miracle fishing spot—the sea, the air—too soon irreversibly blighted, tarnished, contaminated, spoiled. We know the lamenter is justified. We hear the lamenter begging for heated agreement, for moral outrage. No one disagrees—but then what? What second shoe can be made to fall?

Your place or mine? Who gets the parking space?

Place is identity, style, faith, cosmology. For many it dangles a tantalizing, seemingly unreachable ideal. (Shangri-La. Neverland. Mars.) It embodies a partial answer to art's perpetual question *How, then, shall we live?* by replacing the *how* with what may in fact be its most vital component: *where.*

It generates contests—surge upon surge of them, which may simply be low-end versions of tribal battle. Polls are taken; pros and cons weighed: crime rates, taxes, politics, schools, transport, language, jobs, real estate values. *Bien-être* (that slipperiest of slopes: one person's meat, and so on).

We can never accept anyone else's last word. That's part of the endlessness. *We* want the last word. Even if we choose to hang fire we are *thinking* the last word, secretly damned sure we are right.

I've listened quietly while visitors lectured me about places I've lived in for many years. Probably you have, too.

"How dear we hold our perception of the universe," noted Carol Bly in a comment about a Conrad Aiken story. No focus inside that perception is dearer to us, none more urgent, than that of which patch(es) of planet we come from or identify with, and—by consequence—why we intend never to leave, or to which we must return, or why we are hell-bent on getting out of there. Exempting religion and sex, both powerfully influenced by place, what other element so saturates the stories we tell?

When I suggest this, people stare at me as if I'd pinched them—not sure what (if any) rejoinder is called for, except maybe *Well, of course*. My concern seems naïve, floppily amorphous. They mumble, "Uh—yeah." Even given that we can never decide which place may be best, no one seems able to agree on the Godzilla size of our preoccupation: what the great Shirley Hazzard called "the impenetrable phenomenon, which no one, to my knowledge, has ever explained."

The idea, and dream, of Home. How many trillions of words have grappled with it?

Two dear friends, who also happen to be English (not wishing to give the English a bad rap; they're a default family network), argued with my challenge that place may be the only conversation. They reminded me—angrily—that millions of people who are born (and locked) into wretched settings, who'll never have the chance for comparison, can never afford the luxury of thinking about place. As good humanists, my friends felt charged with defending those who had no defenders. Their vehemence hurt me (though they probably did not intend that) and for some time afterward I felt shamed and confused, because I knew my perception contained truth. Then I remembered my early time spent with Peace Corps in Senegal, West Africa. Hard as life was for those kind, wry people, it was clear (from talking and observing) that most dreamed of an Elsewhere, even if it had to be a vague one, pieced together from song lyrics, gossip, or glimpsed photos. Sometimes the harder life was, the more vivid the dream. Writings from individuals who came up in poverty and mayhem, who "alone have escaped to tell thee," bear this out. Often, in a double-knot of paradox, the writer-émigré misses the land she fled, and any number of beloved contemporary writers strive this minute to reconcile, in their work and in their souls, the push-pull of a multiplicity of homes.

All of which brings writers to reflect upon the *where* of our stories. Paraphrasing Gertrude Stein, *where* has a *there*. And that particular *there*, or series of them, tends to be bone-vital to writing.

Readers, for the most part, need location in stories the way humans need it in life. It's an old saw among writers that place functions as character. I'd argue for more: place gives us our own characters back in a kind of bas-relief action, by causing us to notice how we relate to it. I'd argue that place also gives our bodies back to us—the writer's, the reader's—by reminding us that we live in a body. Even as we describe it, place makes us re-feel our physical self and the surfaces it touches: at once a breathing base camp and all that it processes: ground and sky, air and earth; buildings or their ruins, countryside or city, cave or room, lake or sea or trickle from a tap.

Objects. Food. Drink. Other bodies. We're animals, after all.

No doubt plenty of notable works occur to you now in which ethereal (disembodied) sensibilities drift in nothingness; Beckett comes to mind. One could argue that these worlds establish a different set of relational laws, teaching us as we go. No Place is also a place, with a sort of bell jar around it. The writing I like best offers a field against which (upon, through, across, or under which) movement by a set of principals can occur. (Movement, remember, means all versions, including the subtlest *tick*.) Not only does place help convey movement's measure. (Here, then There.) It *interacts* with that measure, imbuing brains and bodies and buildings, everything that is matter, including made-up matter—with tone, color, emotion.

One of the first ways writers find they can winnow into a story, is through the look and feel (sound, smell, taste) of its setting. It may or may not help to travel to the venue where work is set. (Famously, Martin Cruz Smith wrote *Gorky Park* after spending only two weeks in Moscow; Saul Bellow wrote *Henderson the Rain King* without ever placing a foot in Africa). But however particulars are conjured, few skilled writers ignore specifics of place in storymaking. What falls to us—where the art is—is which to select, and when and how to use them.

A confession: as a young reader I used to disdain descriptions of place, rushing through them so I could get to the elements (dialogue, thought, action) I liked better.

Now I slow down, relishing prose depictions of landscape, flora, fauna, buildings and rooms and weather, the way an elderly person might linger over rare photos of family.

And latterly it seems to me more poignant than ironic that the young artist (who leveled the cuts at me about the West) was becoming famous, at the time of his death, for installations that effectively reproduced an American snapshot—a kind of Edward Hopperish, midwestern bleakness—in perfect, dimensional, life-sized detail.

How dear we hold our perception of the universe.

Plato said, "Music is a moral law." Surely place achieves the same. When my sister would murmur, time and again, about the summers where I live, "I could never stand the heat," her words were hushed with moral force. I've spoken with the same awed incredulity to people who've chosen all their lives to endure deep winters, or to dwell in remote outback or amid skyscrapers. We take moral pride—and deep moral umbrage—in the *whys* we build and rebuild, like scaffolding, around our choices of *where.*

As an argument, of course, it will never be settled. But as a driving engine and definition, isn't it strange? As if the first, crudest animal territoriality—the staking of habitat, long before language— had wended its way through millennia of human circuitry, to finally become a mighty entity that looms (like the mysterious, omniscient monolith in *2001: A Space Odyssey*) over our scrappy muddlings, radiating a force field, a portent, a kind of numinousness.

Maybe place controls us because we are made from it, and we feed our remains back to it.

For writers? As hymn, lullaby, anthem—for reflection, for refueling, even for refusal, for defining ourselves away from unhallowed ground—we return again and again to place in the early works that formed us, that delivered place so acutely: White's Arable farm, Brontë's moors, Crusoe's island, Dickens's London, Hugo's Paris, Anderson's Ohio, Cather's Nebraska, McCullers's Georgia, Eloise's Manhattan, Kipling's jungle, Joyce's Dublin, Pasternak's Russia, Doig's Montana, Achebe's Nigeria, Dineson's Kenya, Kincaid's Antigua—millions more, not to mention the unnamed countrysides, forests, villages, and castled kingdoms of fairy tales. To these and all those like them we owe our natures, let alone our writing and reading lives. "There would be no destiny," notes editor Jennifer Acker, "without destination." Stories *are* place. Each sweeps us away. And though we do eventually come back, something is permanently altered. We're remade: slightly different, every single time.

Shake Me Up, Judy

The first thing I do these days, when planning travel, is to not want to go.

Mortal risk, hindrance. Bad idea.

I'm not proud of this unpretty, animal panic, this dumb shuttered obstinacy like a dog's.

There are plenty of reasons for it. They all make sense, in a "life is hard and then you die" way.

You may cut me off; call me grinchy or spoiled. You may remind me that most normal people would sacrifice a body part just to be able to consider—let alone consider abstaining from—the luxury of what is called "leisure travel." In fact I would have been you cutting me off not long ago.

I can only describe a developing languor that intrigues me partly because it is so unpopular.

Everyone loves travel. Everyone is proud of that. Say the words, *We want to travel.* Watch people nod and smile: conspiratorial, intimate, eyeballs glassy. *We're all sophisticates here.* Of course you want to travel. Everyone wants to travel.

Except when, after a while, you don't. Or not so much.

Begin at the beginning.

Travel costs money. Bargaining is seldom an option. You can couch surf and home exchange and redeem flyer miles and take the red-eye, but most treading of foreign surfaces costs money you'd not pay at home. Say, however (and please forgive), that for the moment, modestly, there is adequate money. Travel costs in darker ways. Those interest me.

Call what I am about to describe a form of first-world suffering. But suffering it is—mostly silent, except during fights between individuals shackled together—if scarcely talked about. Mentions of it remain absent from most modern travel writing, and starkly missing—in the sense of *never existed*—from all travel brochures and catalogues of travel gear.

Those pages don't change. Women still look softly dusted with iridescent gold. Tanned men still laugh at something off-camera. Sometimes the models hold a drink, or a chic hat. Or they smile into a smartphone, reading satisfying news. Nowhere seen are the wages of having gotten there: the money paid, the lines waited in, the zero leg room endured, the muzzy loud-speaker announcements of delays and cancellations; stinking bathrooms, screaming babies, sleeping in a crumpled, drooling, malodorous heap on the airport carpet with a protective arm over your bags. No, the models in these photos teleported over. Their bodies are trim, clothing radiantly clean and crisp, faces relaxed. Doubtless they smell terrific. Funniest are photos of handsome couples (*handsome* means people over thirty) paused in sunset light at the rail of a cruise ship. He stands close behind her, arms wrapped around her middle, cheek against her temple. She tilts back against him, her face dreamy. He's triumphant, having arranged (or likely funded) the experience. Both grin toward the horizon, exhilarated. Her diaphanous scarf floats in the ocean wind. His white pants ripple and gleam. *This is it*, their faces tell us, misted eyes suggesting unforeseen thrills. *We did it right.*

Well, that's all a lie.

A traveler's suffering starts after shutting the front door.

Three words: *Everything pushes back.* Like being plunged to the bottom of the sea and told to assemble your respirator and air tank down there. Every effort meets resistance.

We travel expecting something. What we get is something else.

The Unsolvable Thingness of Things

"Pack your bags" used to mean "Get excited." It sounded breath-taking. Objects and clothing we began to assemble felt almost lit from within by magical power.

I think about it differently now. Packing means carrying. Carrying means weight-bearing. Weight-bearing becomes the defining constant that gives accelerating pain. Every physical piece, gossamer as a hankie, weighs. Each item, innocent as milk, adds more. The traveler is forced to miniaturize what's essential. That sounds foolishly obvious—but if the trip is long, beware. For women, laws of space and weight (and security constraints on liquids) promise a personal nightmare, since everything we'll need to live must fit inside the dimensions of a rucksack. (I've had actual nightmares in which I struggled, against that underwater resistance, to gather the right stuff while the deadline for catching my plane bore down.) The tiny spray bottle of scent? Nope. It's extra liquid, plus weight. Washcloth? Alas. It weighs more when wet, needs a small plastic bag (more weight) and, because of that, mildew can set in. Sandals? Exposed toes invite trouble, but above all, shoes add weight. After lugging a pair of sandals, untouched, through all of England and France for five weeks I wanted to burn them, together with the rest of the untouched summer clothing—which I could neither use nor in good conscience dump, nor (expensively) mail home. Asininely, I'd thought September might be warm: another line scribbled onto the long, long list of "never-agains."

Fact is, upon arrival home one wants to burn *everything* one lugged back. The very sight of the stuff—scuffed and stained, stiff with foreign dirt and sweat and detergents—evokes a frantic, crumbly mereness—the shrinking room you crouched in every time you had to decide what to wear each day on the road. The semi-dirty-but-probably-won't-smell-yet thing? The thing that may smell a little but who cares anymore? The thing that never fit, whose stripes have begun to sag? These items stare limp and dull from your battered case. Seeing them again, pulled like dead vermin into the daylight of home, sickens. You can't even stand to see them in *photographs*. Destroy them, donate them, or wash and hide them away for at least a year. Two years is better. I know what I am talking about.

Books become a ball and chain. For we who need books (not devices) like food, this is sorrow. I carry at least one book everywhere anyway—usually two or three. You can't not eat. Or you could, but—no.

Sadly, food itself weighs. *Everything* weighs: tissue, cough drops, earrings.

Even a "light" burden soon grows hateful. Every movement pinches. Consider the two dozen steps leading over all those charming little bridges connecting parts of the delirious glory of Venice to itself. Bags must be schlepped up and down those steps, a million times. The first few times feel rakish. Then the sweat and grit set in. Vaporettos (motorized canoes used as water taxis) cost a fortune. But even if you could afford vaporettos all day, would that really be the best way to encounter the fabled city?

So we schlepp. Grunting, dragging, wrenching, hefting. As Martin Amis noted at the prospect of towing his heavy duffel down the long descent into the London tube: "I can do it . . . but I won't like doing it."

As a result, our relationship to *things* grows extremely strange.

We are made to think very, very hard, I mean molecularly hard, about what we absolutely believe we must have: what we use, wear, consume. The irreducible *thingness* of things becomes an obdurate riddle, like on-screen icons that won't open. Common articles—absurdly modest in the context of home—must be portaged like extra arms and legs, so albatross-like for their sheer awkward constancy they seem to mock us. Again and again we're forced to weigh the stuff's importance against its earthbound weight: the discomfort of hauling versus the comfort of having. This leads to prosecuting oneself for wanting comfort at all, arriving finally at a blank wall of wonder: *what don't I understand about this?* Am I corrupt for insisting on shampoo?

Rick Steves, that buoyant simplifier, bobbing cork of a mascot for American touring, insists it is important to let go of some control, let ourselves run out of toothpaste and shop for it in Bulgaria. But what if we really, really would rather not do that? Does it make us bad?

Product Failure, Stopped Time, Catastrophic Thinking

To travel is to become an astronaut—ambulant, self-sustaining—since there's no guarantee that any stopover, any backdrop, will supply what you need.

But that backdrop, remember, is why you've gone.

You've gone to meet the new. You've gone to place yourself *voluntarily* inside the crunching maw of newness. In many ways it's a video game. Stuff comes at you. Think fast. Duck, parry, deal. No shying away. No tranquil withdrawals, no calm reflection. Oddly, very little privacy comes with travel. You're theatrically visible, *On* with a capital O. You must, navigate, negotiate, be alert—be mindful where you are and who's around and what happens next, forced to make fast deductions and choices that do not (contrary to ads) invigorate. Too bad if you are hungover or sick. Where do we buy tickets? Which kind? How does this machine work? They cost *that much*? Where did you put them? Did we miss our stop? Whose fault is that? Where are we now? Whom should we ask? *You* have the language; *you* start asking.

Often, this is where the bickering begins. I am routinely guilty, it seems, of something called catastrophic thinking—a term supplied by the physical therapist I visited after a sudden, prolonged vertigo attack. At the time of the attack (floors tilting, walls spinning, me vomiting), I feared I was having some life-threatening brain event. It turned out, after tests, to be an unfixable inner-ear event. Meaning I must live with the vertigo (now a vexing but manageable dizziness). Given a life-threatening brain event or vertigo, I'll take the vertigo. But the episode still reminds me how terrified we've all learned to be, defensively, most of the time.

Because—sorry—crazy-awful things happen to people for no reason, all the time. Electing risk, alongside this knowledge, becomes something of an art form.

It's also considered—unfairly and romantically, in my view—a measure of character.

"You're no good in situations like this, are you?" is the accusation I can't deny but hate hearing. It means I'd be the last choice of whom to be stranded with, whom to face problems with. This shames me. Hate accuser, hate self. Lose-lose.

Then the zipper on the ("durable!") travel wallet fails, going off its track. The wallet flops open from its dangling position around your neck, grinning at strangers, exposing all its credit cards, passport, multicolored paper currency. You have to use rubber bands to close it, maneuvering them complicatedly around your wrist while extracting what's needed as the wallet splays shamelessly, flaunting its innards. Husband stares at the broken wallet as if its failure represented some moral lapse of your own. In fact you'd obsessed about purchasing that wallet. In truth, you'd *fetishized* the getting of all your travel gear—researched, analyzed, agonized—finally choosing what you judged would be right.

The right gear, you'd assumed, would make travel easier.

Here is what is true. The little Ryanair-approved carry-on you acquired, in order to avert their drastic fines for outsized luggage, was pleasant—at first—to pull along like a wobbly pet. But it holds so little (a grocery bag's volume) that, desperate for the pathetic few things you feel you *must have*, you pack it too full. It begins to split open.

Like belongings, the body (first and last luggage) starts to show wear that—puzzlingly—you can't remember inflicting. Fingernails break. Feet grow blisters. Elbows sprout patches of rough, scaly skin. Bruises and cuts you have no memory of receiving. Unprecedented rashes. Stomach problems, intestinal problems, viral visits. A patch of lower gum turns meat-red with inflammation. Why now? For what cause? You'll never know. Needless to say, it's twice as miserable being sick on the road as it is being sick at home.

(Souvenir snapshot: Paris's enchanting Pont des Arts on a fall afternoon, the city around us glinting in the sun, my husband standing aside irked and helpless while I'm bent double in coughing fits.)

In fact most of travel's torment proves crushingly physical. Sleep's elusive. Stress is amped. Demands don't slacken just because you're underslept: quite the contrary. Most days you're obliged first thing to jump up, make decisions, run around. You lose control over food and exercise. Eating out, however carefully, means high fat and heavy starch (paradoxically, never filling enough). Your body begins to soften and expand. Midsection and thighs start to feel like wet cotton batting. You can't fasten the top button of your jeans. This makes the fly slide open and they bag down.

"Your jeans are bagging down," your husband points out.

Doing laundry in another country is like trying to do it on another planet, or else as a last resort, bribing someone on that planet to do it for you (uncertain you may ever see your clothes again). Unsurprisingly, dryers in distant lands—if they exist—are weak. Do people there just walk around damp? And thinking about laundry summons another earmark of travel.

Waiting.

Fathomless amounts. Blood-draining eternities. Pointlessness is its punishment.

We know, of course, that time is precious. Time is waning. We should by rights *relish* slowing time. Why then does waiting feel like prison? And what can so much waiting finally mean? Are we secretly waiting for the whole trip to end? Or for the reward—the flash of joy or enlightenment, like the elusive green flash when the setting sun dips into the sea—that all this fuss hoped to spark?

Are we waiting for life to resume?

Or are we waiting for the safe, known life to resume?

Why, on foot, do people thicken around you, blocking your path or clipping you as they speed past, as if choreographed to trip you? (In London we actually stumbled over a woman's lost, single shoe at a mobbed street corner.) This makes you surly. Instead of (as hoped) becoming more sensitive and porous to human plights you morph into a hulking, scowling, forward-pushing shrew with an attitude: angry survivalism. The shift happens animalistically; a primal, preemptive guard. Nerves on red alert have little margin for empathy. Worse, people around you seem to want one of two things: that you get out of their way or you give them money. Often I have felt like a football player running toward the goal (whatever it was) with one hand out to fend off interference.

I, who carry spiders safely out the door rather than kill them.

As noted, I'm not proud of any of this—or of the implication rattling within. What kind of savage am I? Does it take so little to scratch off the humanitarian veneer? What *wouldn't* I do, finally, to get what I want? Whom would I betray?

Enter a hot sense of identity fraud: who we were at home (reasoning, thoughtful, benefit-of-doubt-giving) versus who we become in the airless concrete cell of a stifling Munich hotel in humid summer, where the window won't open more than an inch. Or when young con artists almost (not quite) make off with our wallet in a Paris metro. Or when an unknown guide drives us through a deserted outback in Turkey and we realize we could easily be robbed, killed, and left there with no one any wiser.

You're No Good in These Situations, Are You?

Innocents imagine that travel brings wisdom, that they'll be rocked by electrifying insights as they gaze on exotic vistas. In reality a traveler's thinking lapses into a vacant trance whenever it can, a spaced-out suspension of wits (to give wits time off before the next urgency).

I will allow that travel does also give moments when beauty arrives; beauty so large, so *bouleversant* as to feel like pure revelation—indeed like "all ye need to know."

But these transcendent bits, in my experience, slip away. They're like a concert you recall having been thrilled by though you can no longer remember the music, or even the substance of the thrill. As a writer, I regret this. Writers have an immense stake in their image as *flâneurs* or roving scribes, heading out into blue yonder to soak up material. But rarely have I experienced that quality of rich reflection I once supposed to be a natural byproduct of journeying—the orderly, stately insights flowing from the mouths of Henry James and Somerset Maugham narrators, a depth and acuity only accessible, presumably, while they are "free."

Not for me. Reflection—and its fruit, new understandings—tends to arrive much, much later, in the months and years that follow: in solitude, peace, and perfect privacy.

In the actual moment? A traveler craves relief from constipation or shin splints. She frets about why an ATM won't work, sore and swollen lymph glands, where to print a boarding pass, or (waking with a craggy rock lodged in her throat) whether she has contracted tonsillitis. Or that local pharmacies or ticket counters or grocery stores are closed. Or that she's arrived, with no time to spare, at the wrong terminal. Or that the contemptuous German passport agent now screaming at her may fine her thousands for breaking the Schengen 90-day rule. Or that security personnel in the sleepy Idaho airport will step forward (as she stands innocently in line) to select her for a special test—swiping the palms of her hands with circular white pads that set off alarms on the test machinery because apparently, logically and conveniently, the *hand lotion on the skin of her hands triggers those alarms*, so that she'll be led to an isolated questioning/pat-down center—after which every single thing in her luggage will be removed, and only when officials have satisfied themselves that she and her belongings pose no danger to the American population will she be asked to repack.

(All the above happened.)

It gets stranger.

Together with the fantasy of diving into a well of clear, deep thought, I'd nursed the notion that my own natural sense of apartness—a writer's loneliness—might be rescued by a smarter setting. That is, my sense of alienness in my own country (a hopeless, permanent Quasimodo-ness) would somehow blend perfectly inside another language and different cultural norms—even be cossetted there. To use a lofty analogy: think of James Baldwin in Paris, or Shirley Hazzard in Positano. If my own culture viewed me as a gloomy boho, surely a certain savoir faire elsewhere would recognize, and tend warmly to, the visiting artist.

Instead? Savoir faire zooms past, hell-bent on earning a living, hooking up or breaking up with people, raising kids, finishing school, nailing a job, or finding a nice piece of fish at the market.

A Mysterious Inversion

Going out to eat and staying in hotels no longer seems sexy. That sounds nuts. But after enough time in transit, something inverts. What was once special and luxurious looms as an exhausting rip-off. Why? Because we're strapped to it, confined to it, condemned to repeat it. We begin to see too much: dirt, mold, sullen employees, troubling smells. For salt in the wound, these venues tend to be wildly overpriced. The theater of them feels tragicomic; we're embarrassed for our parts in perpetuating it. The waitress who takes our coffee order is thin, breathless, curt. The freshness of morning does not sing to her. *Je vous écoute*, she says crisply (*I'm listening*), pad and pen readied. *No funny stuff* is the icy message. *Don't hang your drippy ideas on me.* The young man setting the salad before us that evening looks tired and distracted, as does the clerk at the lobby desk and the empty-eyed maid brushing past. They have bosses to appease, bills to pay, babies to bear. The hotel's back stairs are grimy. The sticky service entrances, trashed alleyways, weirdly rigged toilets, tangled wiring—all the backstage of it worms into consciousness. Workers on break huddle outside, smoking, desolation stamped on their faces.

The vision has cracked. It is leaking.

What don't I understand about this?

Mortal Reverb, Cellular Memory, and the Unanswerable Question

As countdown to departure looms, if you are planning to travel far, those dear to you begin to look more precious, a bit shrunken. You search their eyes. They search yours. Everyone is choked by something no one dares name. The surrounding air in those moments grows still.

It's mortal terror. The act of going away removes us, with no guarantee of return—imitating its metaphorical brother, sleep: a *petit mort*, a little death. Now we have the specter of a half-dozen world capital massacres to decorate our imaginations. But the ethos of *Travel Trumps All* stands tough, indestructible (externally at least). No one slaps departing friends on the back and cracks *don't forget to avoid suicide bombers* in the same way they might chime *don't forget your phone charger* or *don't forget to text*. Yet we invest farewell celebrations with unspoken, ghoulish significance: this may be the final good-bye.

Alright then. Why do it? Why go?

I have asked that question, of myself and others, ten thousand times.

When I was young and poor and feckless, no such question occurred to me. Without a flicker of hesitation, travel on any terms was snatched up. I'd go anywhere on a dime—and I never had more than a handful of dimes. I went to West Africa with the Peace Corps, ate and drank and sang and wept with my co-volunteer all very young women like me who (like me) fell in hopeless love with our handsome Senegalese language instructors and who (like me), once installed out in the bush, often spent a lot of time squatted over a makeshift hole in the earth (courtesy of amoebic dysentery), looking up at the vast African sky filled with pinpoint stars. All this was carried off with easy fatalism. (Dysentery was a nuisance, but we were immortal.) Years later my then-boyfriend and I, between rentals, slept in a pup tent on pastureland halfway up a Hawaiian volcano. A cow liked to lean against the tent to scratch itself in the morning. We stashed our few belongings in the tiny storage pocket behind the back seat of my old Volkswagen Bug and washed in local gas station restrooms. Later we stowed away to the island of Tahiti on a flight chartered for a soccer team, and slept our first night in Papeete in a public park. I woke at dawn to find the park's French security guard stretched full length beside me, wistfully running a hand ever so lightly along my exposed leg. (No harm done. I woke my boyfriend; we gathered ourselves groggily and raced away; the guard sat up smiling, sheepish.)

It's startling to look back upon that young woman now. What most touches me is her spirited "yes" to everything. You simply got on with the adventure in those years, whatever it was, however you could. That was the mandate. No blame, no whining, no equivocating. There wasn't even a half-baked mission statement, just a cheerful, practical *onwardness*. More touchingly, beneath that I see, like strong bones in an X-ray, the core assumption—not belief but assumption, the way we assume the fact of air—that all these wanderings were important. All had meaning.

My husband remains, even at our late ages, much like my younger self. He grew up so poor in the industrial north of England that his family could never afford to go anywhere very far from its depressed mill town. He'd show his parents brochures for warm, pretty places. They'd shake their heads. The best they could offer were small drives to the city of Manchester's airport, to watch planes come and go. (The first suntan my husband ever saw was that of Prince Philip, who popped through town on the way back from visiting his native Greece.) Maybe it's not surprising, then, that my husband would gleefully be packed and ready to fly to the moon in fifteen minutes if asked; he'll sleep in a hammock and eat a bowl of gruel-drizzled rice if that's all there is *en voyage*. He rushes now to arrange each next trip—often a year in advance.

I understand his reasoning. It's everyone's mantra, words people love to fondle and recite on cue.

That it's good for us.

Good to be forced to push, especially when it's hard. Good to be uncomfortable, to solve or fix or cope. Good to be stone-mystified.

Good to wade into difficulty, strangeness, humbug. Good to see new stuff, to struggle. Good for the brain, good for the body. *Oh, right. We're alive.*

Brain and body waken, as well, to the fact of Others: their decency. This comprehension, for me, is probably the central gift of travel. Despite everything, most people are focused on staying upright, caring for themselves and their families. These tasks are visibly harder outside America, even in posh capitals, and travel always reminds us of the comparative luxury of our own lives. The arbitrariness of our luck brings a moral undertow: how should we live in response to that? In *responsible* response, that is.

Somehow, the cells remember everything. This is not quite related to the whatever-doesn't-kill-you model. It may be closer to a trope expressed by the character Mr. Smallweed in Dickens's *Bleak House.* Smallweed is a venomous but curiously vital man whose unnamed illness keeps him stuck, semi-supine, in a chair. His body is old and rotting. When he wants freshened clarity he orders his strong, grown granddaughter, who obediently moves behind him, "Shake me up, Judy!" She gets her upper arms under his armpits from behind, and proceeds to lift and turn his torso while administering a good hard series of downward shakes. You can hear the crack and pop of rearranging bones.

And yet.

I can no longer buy the stock sales pitch, the hearty *take your weird-tasting travel medicine and become a better person* bromide. It's too pat. One size may not fit all.

Why the Bear Went over the Mountain

Facts? Travel beats us up. It's shockingly expensive. Its effects upon the planet, and upon those we visit, are ecologically and morally questionable. It takes a chunk of time to recover. (The cells remember *that,* too.) There is also, floating over these concerns like a polluted cloud, the troubling fact of a scarcity of human interpenetration. That is, most tourists are routinely buffered first to last by a sealed environment, so that their "trip" consists of acting out in familiar ways, in familiar language, against a borrowed landscape. (If you have ever lived in a resort destination, you have dwelled in the graphic, daily evidence of this.)

Other tourists make a prideful mythology of travel ordeals: "It happened this way, which proves that I am right about what is real." Though telling stories later is not strictly why we go. (No one is listening for long, immersed as they are in their own stories.)

We go, I think, driven by combined ennui and curiosity, for the same reason the bear went over the mountain: *to see what we can see*—meaning, to my thinking, what we are able (physically and spiritually) to discern and to name, flavored by who we are in the moment of seeing; what shape and strength of mind and soul we bring to it. What we see will forever inform everything we think, say, and do, including (if we are looking carefully) a fresh understanding of our own potential barbarism, our fearful, greedy parts. We know more, respect more, are humbled by more—most of all by what we don't understand.

I am uneasy, however, letting that argument plant its smug flag there and dust its hands.

Why should anyone's aversion to risk and discomfort, particularly as they age, automatically translate as weakness of spirit? Emily Dickinson seldom left her house. Proust, in the habits of his person, was not exactly an action figure. While we live, there's no report card. After we die, there are only platitudes. Why not, in what time remains, do more of what we like to do and less of what we don't? In the same way that perceptions refine with age, why shouldn't tastes?

An aging east coast friend, a shrewd and vibrant writer, once told me she was embarking on a brief getaway to a small Italian town with her (eighty-something-year-old) boyfriend—and that while there she meant to try her best "not to learn anything."

That little aside shocked me a minute. Then it flooded me with delight. I still delight in it when I think about the great *earnestness* of most Americans—me foremost among them. American earnestness often seems a kind of solipsistic apple-polishing, a shiny dream of self-in-the-world, a story we tell ourselves, while stepping off the cliff, about who we are and (for that matter) that the world cares.

It also enables us—strangely—to do things we did not know we couldn't.

Or shouldn't.

What I finally suspect about my growing dismay is that it springs from a common condition not limited to age: Weltschmerz, defined online as "melancholy" and "world-pain" or "world-weariness." It may not be something to brag about. It's also a solid element of art that people recognize with relief, even elation—think of flamenco or blues—because it makes them feel less alone. Wikipedia describes the word as originating with a German author who declared that Weltschmerz "denotes the kind of feeling experienced by someone who believes that physical reality can never satisfy the demands of the mind."

We travel expecting something. We get something else.

"Everything," said a wise man to me once, when I was young and arrogant, "is exactly what you hold it to be." We are free to create meaning, free to change it. The stories we tell ourselves will be as real as needed, until the next story bumps it. Experience will bear out what we wish it to. Travel is a luxury, an emblem of courage or pluck, an edifying, sometimes life-changing milestone. Travel is a deluded, vain, superficial, exhausting, costly business, bad for the planet's health and soon forgotten by its perpetrators—ultimately, by everyone.

So why is not easier, I wonder, to "snap out of" Weltschmerz?

One guess is that it's pure biology—an organism's life-force slowing. But right up in our faces, generations of artists do their best work in their sixties, seventies, eighties, even nineties. (Pablo Casals, asked why he was still practicing the cello in his nineties: "Because I think I'm making progress.") Everything is what we hold it to be.

If the fault, then, is strictly a failure of imagination, why can't I just will a reversal? The truth makes such a buzzkill. *I don't travel well anymore.* There it stands: homely, inexcusable.

But will I volunteer that to the young people in my life?

Never.

My granddaughters are in their teens; a stepson and nephews in their twenties and thirties. Some are starting families, a slew of new little ones. All have to live through the events and interactions that will form them. That's sacred stuff to discover, consider, revisit, tweak, and reflect upon along the continuum of time—like one of those moving walkways at the airport. The walkway is a constant for all of us; the only variable being where, along its spectrum, we happen to stand.

For the young, understanding through the eyes, ears, nose, and guts that the rest of the world really exists is no small thing—maybe even vital to the making of a moral citizen. When people say Buenos Aires or Bangkok or Pago Pago, it's crucial for the young to know—in their bodies—that these are not just words but homes to fellow beings, their lives and dreams.

I will lock away my own embattled weirdness and tell my young family there's no more passionate, no more permanent an education than travel. That's *all* I will tell them, and it won't be a lie. Everyone—but especially the young—deserves a shot at going to see what they can see. *Adventure* is still a sturdy word, and the vision it evokes from old Latin and French—*a thing about to happen*, or better yet, *what must happen*—is still delicious. I will urge them to be sane, avoid war zones. But I will urge them to get out there. They won't need (or want) to hear my own, privately weary tune, as I keep eyeballing those ads for a durable travel wallet popping up in the margins of my computer screen. The manufacturers make many claims for the product these days: slash-proof, waterproof, scan-proof, grab-resistant, and—they assure me—secure zip closure.

Cake-Frosting Country

1.

If you've not yet seen it, I can tell you this. Everything you've heard is true.

The cake-frosting countryside. The train streaming through fields of green or gold, past white cows, rows of vegetables, sunflowers, lavender, orchards, vineyards. Umber-roofed towns and villages huddled at mid-distance, like illustrations for fairy tales. Farmhouses from earlier centuries; the occasional castle or its ruins, crown passing hills. Rivers wend blue-green, peaceful, like backdrops of Renaissance paintings. At the north, Brittany, cold and briny, stoic. At the south, the Côte D'Azur, a flat, warm bath of heart-piercing blue. And in the upper middle of the hexagon (as it nicknames itself), like the beating heart of the world, the city of Paris.

Nowhere in this dream, unless you are a corrosively tempered critic, can you find a bite of bad food.

The further miracle? It's all pretty much still there.

Some will argue that it is changing, and not for the better. Fine. Let them cuddle their perfectly defensible objections, and go elsewhere.

The glory of being an older writer—fortified by the flexible essay form—is that one needn't justify much. I claim no historic or cultural expertise. My language skills, while helpful and pleasurable (about which, more in a moment), are mild. We haven't bought a house or apartment and begun the long toil of ingratiating ourselves.

Apart from a couple of acquaintances, I have no insider contacts, no professional connections. But I've spent modest intervals of time in France over a span of years, and as a wise friend once summarized it, "They do many things very well."

What is harder to measure, harder to convey, is how one learns to see differently—sees oneself differently—with each visit. Gone, certainly, is the early romance, the breathless Rilkean *you must change your life* striking full force as you stand trembling in the street while the old church chimes the hour in the dim, freezing dusk. As a young adult, one is convinced that those church chimes and that Rilkean resolution have been handed down directly, like God's instructions to Noah. The ancientness of the country's very earth staggers us. The cold stone and mummified wax of cathedrals; the shop windows filled with old framed drawings or inexplicable masks, with entrails, bread, violins, lingerie, or sleeping cats; the exquisite harp or guitar or steel drum or jazz bass concerts from starving artists in the *métro* labyrinths; the musical *bong* of announcements in the noisy, pigeon-festooned train stations—all of it stings with portent, a hard slap. You wander, those first visits, in a state of penitent wonder.

Penitent for what? For not having understood sooner: Here was a way to live.

In latter visits, the experiences remain (again, miraculously) much the same. But the understanding is wearier. My face, in photographs, shows this. Whether one lives or dies, believes oneself happy or not, the cold will be cold; the heat pitiless; the chimes will chime. It is unlikely one will change one's American life. The encumbering nature of that life—numbing job, witless errands, too few margins—supplies the time and money to enable these visits. (Escape velocity, we call it.) But it seems no small awareness—at least, not to me—that when time and money are somehow corralled for it, France is where I want to go.

All one need do, for context, is fan out a series of visuals like a deck of cards. And it isn't strictly beauty one exalts, though that wouldn't be wrong, but rather a beauty that leads into the larger understanding. Olives, cheeses, nuts, oils, fish, tomatoes, gleaming like jewels, are part of that understanding. So are *rôti* chicken, turkey, or lamb turning on the spit; white beans or small, red potatoes basting in their juices. Chattering kids fleeing school, gesturing with a *pain au chocolat* or baguette. The taste of the first kir (dry white wine or champagne with a dash of blackcurrant cordial) in early evening. Nannies and young mothers shepherding toddlers with the same reprimands we've heard over a lifetime: *C'est quel façon de parler?* (What kind of way is that to talk?) *Tu t'as lavé les mains?* (You washed your hands?) Pregnant women: graceful, insouciant, as erotically beautiful as any you'll ever see. Women of a certain age (my own) giving the nightly television weather forecasts (*Météo*), flushed and charmed as though they'd just risen, on a whim, from a dinner-party table. And even in the rougher, messier, working-class towns and districts, the unimpeachable dignity of the lone figure, man or woman, at a meal: the book or newspaper, the coffee, the snifter of Armagnac.

The streets, the crowds, the secret courtyards, your aching shins, the youths clattering at top speed down a stairwell, giving you a wink.

C'est sportif! they shout.

2.

It began, my husband notes, with topsoil.

A great glacial push from the East sent it westward, stacking it sixteen feet deep upon the lucky hexagon. And though its climate and topography vary madly, a line drawn across its middle delegates destiny. North and south yield logical products of their geographic données—butter above, olive oil below; white wines and champagne above, Bordeaux and varietal reds below (berries that have to *work* to exist)—for all of which we are, without question, better.

Let's now review some of the standard waivers and qualifiers.

The visitor, of course, perceives her dream from a buffered

status of every stripe. We've put up the money to be there. We never had to apply for a job, install a phone, get something fixed. The country, bolstered by travel companies and entertainment media, serves as (far and away) the world's most-visited tourist destination, and certainly the biggest repository for romantic projection. If you made a bulleted list of national problems, it would run long: Lack of social mobility. Top-heavy power and snobbery. Enormous economic barriers to new businesses, to enterprise and initiative. Taxes must be paid *before* income is earned; they're high. Everyone works for the state. Getting hired is nearly impossible, since it's nearly impossible to be fired. A problematic education system. The country's soccer team is in decline. This list won't lack for evidence of bizarre difficulty, cruelty, strangulation by red tape, injustice, racial strife, want, sorrow, bitter provincialism, ruthless political exploitation, and weird, inscrutable annoyances. Elevators are often very old, cramped as a phone booth. They rattle threateningly as they struggle up and down, and when they break, woe to you. One plays hopscotch avoiding dog shit on the sidewalks. Strikes (*grèves*) are so pandemic that on any given day, one or another group essential to the social and economic bien-être is likely to be blockading the highway and dumping milk, oranges, or tires into the gutters.

Toilets—dodgy.

Now let's celebrate some of the Many Things Done Well.

Infrastructure is terrific: roads, bridges, and public transport among the best. Stability is a bragging point: social and economic fabric holds steady. When you go, years later, to revisit your favorite shop or eatery or bookstore, odds are excellent that it remains where you remember it, run by the same people, who own the same *pets*. Extreme care is taken with food and wine—little or no genetic meddling, few or no pesticides. Almost anything tastes (for those who grew up that long ago) like your earliest memory of it. Wine is delicious, kindly priced, wholesome and fundamental as milk. Costs of services are socialized, allowing more people access not only to excellent food and health care but also to art, music, theater, dance. (We saw the play *Ubu Roi* at the palatial Comèdie Française for about $15 each.) Housing and jobs, food, streets, and most public services are maintained remarkably well.

People, for the most part, are courteous, witty, helpful. Many go out of their ways to assist. When I thanked one woman, she laughed: "You'd do it for me in San Francisco." What has most consistently struck me, of all I've witnessed there, is the special, sane civility with which the French carry on living. They work, buy groceries, take their kids to lunch and look over their school-work. They peruse bookstores, libraries, galleries. They use their parks. They adore picnics—invented them, it's said. Students con-stantly organize *manifestations* (demonstrations or be-ins), some-times just for the joy of partying. Nastier occasions occur, of course, but one learns to absorb these with an amused fatalism, exempli-fied (visibly and famously) by the French themselves.

To be amid beautiful architecture—monuments, mansard rooves, *hôtels particuliers*—is to be made larger, and better, in a stroke. (Imagine a full-scale coliseum, three blocks from an immac-ulate Roman temple, smack in the middle of the modestly sized city of Nîmes.) Each building, whether ancient, nineteenth century, or modern, presents not just a work of art but a kind of *philosophi-cal proposition into which the gazer is invited*—to linger, ponder; edge toward an idea. To walk street after street—looking out to the Louvre, the d'Orsay, the Academie française, the bridges, quays, statuary, fountains—is to feel one's knees buckle: not only trying to assimilate the vision, itself a suggestion of the very best our species might be capable of, but also with the rather stunning sense of one's own boundaries (identity, sensibility) swimming apart, breaking up, diffusing in a universe more infinite, more dazzling than any her mind had posited until that moment.

You go with every pore open to it.

3.

Americans are never easy in their minds about the French. We are intimidated, confused, piqued. Never was this better satirized than by television's *Saturday Night Live*, whose bald, pointy-headed space-alien family (the Coneheads) instructed its children to tell the curious that "we are from France." Most often, however, Americans (with other affluent, westernized cultures) are a culture of appropriators. *Done it; got it.* Everyone has his or her France, his or her Paris, just as everyone has his or her London or New York. This stubborn habit strikes me as self-protection, an old tribal instinct for never showing one's back. Not knowing, not having gotten there first (and pocketed the goods), seem to implicate us as fools or rubes.

Nonetheless, the realist understands that to travel is to agree to be a fool awhile. A traveler relinquishes much control, and does humbling work. It's part of the bargain, and it's good for us. The late Harvard philosopher George Santayana declared, in an essay called "The Philosophy of Travel," that we "need sometimes to escape . . . into the moral holiday of running some pure hazard, in order to sharpen the edge of life . . ." One is tested: standing in lines, confronting the sour clerk, stranded by another grève. Yet anger seems to evaporate with the next lovely view, the next meal, the softness of the air.

I've worried that tourism helps contaminate that which one loves. But it can never be entirely so. Too many bridging incidents—conversations, laughter, exasperation over trifles—affirm that *on se comprend*: if only a fragile strand, for an instant, we understand each other. Shirley Hazzard, in a long-ago article for the *New York Times Magazine* about her second home—Naples— suggests what is necessary:

One needs leisure; one needs imagination. And something more: vulnerability. Vulnerability to time interleaved; to experiences not accessible to our prompt classifications . . .

Books feed this quest, and the mystique itself. Random titles come to mind—MFK Fisher's reminiscences of her years there, *Two Towns in Provence* and *Long Ago in France*; Adam Gopnik's account of his young family's Paris sojourn, *Paris to the Moon*; Alice Kaplan's spellbinding memoir, *French Lessons*; David

Sedaris's send-up of a nonspeaker's perceptions, *Me Talk Pretty One Day*; Lily King's addictive novel about a young American au pair in a French family, *The Pleasing Hour*. My husband just finished Graham Robb's *The Discovery of France*, a revelatory "historical geography." Jean Valjean and Jean Genet, Balzac and Brookner, Stendahl and Sartre: all whet our longing to peek under that opalescent veneer of the Other. And the French Other can prove trickier, let's stipulate for the moment, than any *other*.

4.

The project applies, as well, to language.

I began studying French in high school, loving its sound, its capacity for smoky nuance, its wit and grace. I continued in college, using what I'd learned in West Africa during a Peace Corps stint. Then I let it float, marshalling it for occasional travel; seeking piecemeal recordings, periodicals, films. My relationship to the language is that of a scorned lover, requiring incessant, alert attention. Listening, I often "read" from an invisible ticker tape unspooling: if people rattle on too fast, the tape becomes a blur. If things go well there's no ticker tape; the meaning simply opens inside my consciousness, just as English meaning will. After a day of translation I feel dazed and clumsy, but the language seduces me again and again: advertisements, street signs, eavesdropping. Its enunciation and modulation tantalize my ear like musical bells; in my throat and mouth the words are lozenges, smooth, rich, reverberant. Each time a stranger apprises in passing, *But you speak very well, madame*, my heart quickens. I don't want to *be* them: I have wits enough to understand that. But I long to be at ease with the language, to shape and parry with the deftness I take for granted in English. That, I know, takes years of immersion. Yet I persist *au hasard*, in stabs. To paraphrase Alice Kaplan in *French Lessons*, the language isn't an accomplishment, so much as a need.

I have a friend (disguised here) whose French is a native's, and who translates modern French writers, working, as a day job, for an embassy office. I never spoke much French at the parties he threw for his colleagues, not only because I felt self-conscious, but because I sensed he did not want me poaching in his territory. Though someone in his crowd told him she thought I was French (a tingle of pleasure shot through me to hear that), the feeling stuck. Once he spoke to me of a new novel he was about to translate. And because I sometimes read work in the original French—horribly slowly, with a dictionary in hand—I asked whether he thought I might try this one.

"Oh, no. I don't think so." He frowned, shaking his head. "It's very complicated."

I felt amazed. There was no law, to my knowledge, barring Americans from buying the book, which was a huge hit at the time in France. (A vibrant literary culture thrives there.) I'd be the last to disrespect the translator's art. (Alice Kaplan considers it deeply in "Translation: the biography of an artform," Mots Pluriels no. 23, March 2003, accessible online.) My friend was claiming superior awareness, insights into the elusive French sensibility I could never, apparently, attain. Though I'd loved Annie Ernaux and Flaubert in the original, perhaps my friend was right. Still, I remained astonished by his dismissal.

Then one recent afternoon a retired coworker dropped into my day-job office. A pleasant, cheerful man, he and his wife had decided to vacation in France. His wife, he noted with pride, spoke a bit of French; she was brushing up with tapes and CDs.

I said nothing, while I listened to my brain hiss at this man: You deluded sod; you can't possibly appreciate what you're about to see. She can't possibly convey the language properly. You can't value the history, the art, the glittering tableaux, the Rilkean lightning bolt, the flavor of overheard commentary. How will you honor the sad smile of the woman in the opposite métro seat during the umpteenth grève, as the car halts in darkness, who responded (when I begged to know how she could bear it), "We are a moribund people"?

My France. *My* French.

Cake-Frosting Coda

The Astonishment Index

Someone close to me recently suggested, about the work of a famous living poet, that everything she writes is an expression of shock—arising from the thunderbolt comprehension of the fact that we will die.

That shock evokes—rather, tugs like an attached cart after itself—the ancillary question of how then to live, how to be, during our brief tenure of time on earth.

It strikes me increasingly that we never really recover from this first astonishment: that it extends vastly from and through our lives, like spokes of a wheel.

It strikes me too that everything we say and do, once that double-whammy realization cracks open, is driven by it. Perhaps more strangely, the fact of Place feels intimately bound up with the whole business—this acute, spreading recognition of a finite self, operating so briefly in time and space.

We wonder not just how to be, but why—and, inevitably, where.

It's arguable that my American generation, post–World War II, was saddled with a sanitized moral vision—a series of givens about fairness, or at least of eventual tit-for-tat. We were taught to do good, and we expected that good would be offered back to us in return. We were encouraged to reason, never questioning the (hard-won) modicum of food and shelter enabling this luxury: food, shelter, and a resuming moral order, furnished by a shaken adult population doing its best to rebuild in the wake of unspeakable horror.

So when we grew up and began to travel to the classic world capitals, we viewed them through a rosier lens—possibly a Disney-ized lens, of princesses and castles and kindly old shoemakers. (Later we applied the Jamesian/Kerouacian lenses: *"Live all you can; it's a mistake not to."*) A piquant paradox: how my own great-grandparents, and those of countless others, likely fled Europe for Ellis Island, and how their progeny's progeny eventually returned to Europe as self-styled rogues and daring artist-adventurers (never mind the exciting new venue's dark history). This imposed romance, in effect appropriating a backdrop, persists to some degree in our own kids—though I think that it probably peaked in my own generation; that young adults now, chafed by the bizarre trials of making their own lives (paying off loans), look coolly at any notion of Dharma bumming (unless someone else is funding it).

I recently revisited France, starting in a small, sleepy southern town and moving north to Paris, the journey viewed this time through a pair of eyes seasoned by inevitabilities of age— windfalls and personal loss: books published, babies born, the death of an only, beloved sibling. And while *L'Hexagone* delivered everything described in my prior essay about the cake-frosting country, those real joys felt limned this time by deepened tensions and frailties. All the jewels remain intact in the crown, but they seem to have shrunk a little. Life feels tougher there, more fraught. North African storekeepers look grimmer, more vigilant; teenagers act out more recklessly; clerks, street people, business types, even nannies all seem tightened, more pinched by want and need as they move through the day's obligations. A certain playfulness seems to have vanished. Everything is bewilderingly expensive. True, restaurants and cafes still bustle with people who appear poised, accomplished, at ease with the world and with their meal's bill. But waitstaff, as they hustle about, damp and breathless, exude a telling, desperate fatigue. The divide between haves and have-nots grows starker.

This, too, counts as astonishment.

If we are honest with ourselves about it, we're never ready for the next revelation, whether for good or for ill. It falls to an individual's habits of thought—an inborn or willed resolve—to be able to witness the rise and fall of empires and ideals; to live with surging change and uncertainty and knit meaning from them; to carry on with what remains. Part of what is gained with age is a richer sense of how little these parsings (and the parser him- or herself) finally matter. France does not care who loves or hates it, just as any piece of timeless music or art does not care.

Do I still champion the cake-frosting country? Yes, but with an asterisk—an existential qualifier, an expressive shrug in the best Gallic tradition: "as it stands, as best one can."

In Case of Firenze

Banishing the Voices

See the mouths open before you finish telling them you're going.

Watch the breath being drawn. Watch the lecture-on-the-brink fire their gazes:

(Here is what you should do. Here is what you must see. There's where you'll find the darling old couple who will cook you the Renaissance Special. This is the exact street and stall and name to ask for and what you must understand to the roots or you cannot possibly claim to know anything about it.)

(Here is what you must think and feel about this ancient, compressed dream of red-tiled roofs and mustard and rust, salmon-pink ochre, cocoa, café crème, Roman archways showing through in patches, fading frescoes across marble. Chunks of felled columns. Seven bridges over a brown river boiling through town day and night throwing light; cold mist cloaking the air; palazzos aligned like tired dowagers reporting to duty. Dark, icy museums packed with dusty reliquary. Long, sorrowful windows, splintering shutters. Towers of mossed stone buttressed by a sea of Tuscan green; carved passages surging with anthill traffic, cavalcades of light.)

Listen to *I envy you.*

Followed by *You have not lived unless you (—). You cannot comprehend the place, cannot be worthy of it, unless you (—).*

Wonder why it must be this way.

Decide it has to do with stories we tell, with ownership, winning, first dibs. Curators of authentic life as opposed to artifice—those frayed, throwaway copies everywhere else.

Now banish those voices to their own time zone.

Thank God you have no phone.

Let the voices fade as they call the place their *second home*, claim every speck of history, pageantry, secret rooms and hidden churches and elite villas and locked-away masterpieces in private passageways opened for ten minutes to three people once per year.

Run away.

You are free. Go out to the streets. Wade in.

Try to get lost.

The River

Take an apartment on the Arno in winter: very cold. The building is old—every building is old—seven hundred years. Hear all the plumbing. Hear voices echo in the cement stairwell. Once it was someone's family palazzo: every building was someone's palazzo. Rush to stare out each window. Stand hypnotized by the glittering river, color of mud if mud were a paste made of greenish stone, branches and debris rocketing along. See the silken light from the water shiver on your bedroom ceilings, walls, window frames, light the color of champagne: there it will bobble and shimmer all day.

Mark how the river swells in rain, seethes and rushes, browner with fresh mud, ragged lines of foam, seagulls diving above it, trying to snatch from each other whatever is fished up.

When the church bells start, decide it sounds like the end of a long and terrible war.

Faces

Start a mental list of categories. Long, pale, solemn. Dark and burning. Bone structures of models, statuary, old paintings, Julia Margaret Cameron photos. The gaunt storekeeper, standard beige-red-black plaid scarf around his neck, poking his head out to peer down the Lung'arno. The old woman in the red coat hunched forward, hands clasped behind as she advances like a bent bird. Notice how the eyes retreat, opaque as the river, freighted, blue-black arcs circling them like rainbows around the moon. Brown and fair, ghostly and private. Proud, wounded, preoccupied, in complicated haste. Discern how beauties of both sexes focus on the middle distance, as if to say *Something is needed. Something is missing.* Believe them.

Mistake

Read *Room with a View* first thing, even though you read it long ago. Loathe it this time. Find it foppish, arrogant, a farce of archaic manners, the moneyed English as bumbling leaders pitying a crude, childlike, straw-specked peasantry. Feel ashamed of con-quering cultures, especially your own. Feel sad about Forster, whom you'd once thought understood everything. He was only twenty-nine at the time, but still.

Dogs

Find them homely, small and matted, cataract blind, white whis-kered, half mad. Feel baffled that a world of humans devotes itself tenderly to them. Feel badly about your own meanness—at home, you love dogs—but unable to stanch it because they're crazy here; their eyes dull as murderers'. Watch them hurl themselves at the dividing glass in doorways and store windows, yelping like starved feral things. Notice them lunge at each other, leashed, roaring, to the point of hanging themselves when they pass each other. Watch their owners struggling to hold them apart, smiling and murmuring as if they find this display touching and rather marvelous, often dressing the dogs in sweaters, T-shirts, raincoats, ski jackets. See how beggars put wool caps on them and a cup for spare change beside them with a hand-lettered sign in Italian: *I'm hungry too.*

Presume the bigger dogs are smarter because they are calmer—
the occasional Newfoundland or St. Bernard in the Piazza Signo-
ria, the dignified retriever escorting a mother and two small sons.
Assume these dogs feel pleased to dwell in a climate where fur is
comfortable. Admire their fluent Italian.

Discover almost no cats. Feel unsurprised.

In the courtyard of the building next door, inspect the runty
mutt allowed outside its apartment two or three times a day, so
maddened by the implications of fresh air that it stands still, takes
a few steps, and screams: a sound like an air horn combined with a
slaughtered animal's bleat. Call the dog horrible names aloud.
Invite it aloud, in X-rated language, to cease to exist. Review cinematic fantasies of cooking it for dinner.

Pay strict attention to the matter of feces, which appears daily
on the sidewalks. Look away from your feet only at quick intervals.
Thank heaven and fate and custom that the city hoses down its
streets every morning.

Joggers

Observe them day and night, in cold and rain and sun, young to
late-middle-age, all shapes, sizes, and styles, trotting through
streets and parks in spandex and electronic earpieces, calling
encouragement to each other: *Eh, ragazzi, forza, forza!*

Feel a moment's envy. Then remember that walking all day (and
half the night) is plenty.

Herds and Brigades

Face Japanese tour groups pouring like loud sand into every corridor of the city, moving in mobs, eating and photographing and nat-
tering in mobs. Watch them trail each other for miles in anxious
procession as if from a Bergman film, expensive cameras garland-
ing necks and hands, dolls and stuffed animals tied to backpacks.
Try to figure out why some of the women dress like 1920s flappers,

or little girls. Lose interest. Notice that men and women wear surgical masks. Float the idea that for them no experience is real, no object exists, until photographed. Note that none interacts with the city or its features or denizens, except by camera. Watch them standing before a sculpture or painting, a flotilla of sprouted arms raising smartphones high as if in Fascistic salute.

Overhear someone say that the surgical masks are worn to keep from spreading germs to *others*. Process this as a mild revelation, but lapse back into sourness as each new mob rounds a corner, shouting, bearing down upon you.

Remind yourself that Americans exhibit all the above behaviors. Remind yourself that for that matter, Italians run in rampant herds and screech the roof off.

And yet.

Food

Insist at the beginning that Italian food may be the most wonderful on earth because it is simple and fresh. Feel a corollary pang that because you walk all day, you can never eat enough.

Arrive at these descriptions: that an egg tastes like your earliest memory of egg. That chicken, if scrawny, explodes with flavor, skin crisp and crackling. That cheeses and salamis, hot-roast pork piled in slices with a pinch of salt between two simple halves of bread, some of the crisp fatty skin left on deliberately—likewise pepperoni, prosciutto, pancetta, little quiche-like tarts of spinach or onion or *carciofi*—make you want to whimper. That pesto *alla mamma* explodes on the tongue. That fruit and vegetables sparkle and taste worlds better than their counterparts from even the most expensive food boutiques in America. Worship daily at the shrines of shining purple eggplant; carciofi eaten whole; broccoli, red onions, radiant greens, giant peppers striped in rainbow hues; clementines; strawberries. Tomatoes like no others. Apples, blood oranges, pears tasting of honey.

Asked if an item is good, the fruit seller strokes her cheek once with a forefinger. It means "killer."

Learn quickly that restaurant meals present problems because tourism forces them to make dismal adaptations: bored, weary staff, undistinguished food served in small amounts, sometimes cold, often absurdly expensive. Feel sluttishly willing to look past much of this because *finocchiona*, (salami containing fennel) is to die for. Conclude that since markets spill with beautiful food at low cost, one must take home and cook every treasure: fish, meats, fowl, greens.

Fixate, dazed, on the gorgonzola in a small tub, doled out with a spatula, olives shining in multiple colors.

Note that market sellers are patient and gracious. Sometimes they sing.

Glimpse something flinty, just visible, flickering behind their patience.

Birds

Let your eyes follow gulls and geese sailing over the river. See them hover low, to fish. Do the same with flocks of starlings; the lone egret, a white treble clef against the brown banks; pigeons of every color and mannerism; ducks traveling in families, leaving a wide V on the river in their wake; blackbirds, street-tough, noisy and skinny. A single gray heron, gliding upriver. Chickadees flutter and fight in the courtyard next door, hopping in and out of the tiny house built for them, chittering. It has holes for doors, a single red tile for its roof.

Wonder whether the birds sleep in the late afternoons—but no, look: there they are.

Beggars

Notice the uniform: like Russian peasants, long velvet skirts, ski jackets, kerchiefs, socks with sandals. Begin to recognize them as individuals, each patrolling a zone. Perhaps the mayor or his henchmen, or the carabinieri or *Polizia*, have cut a deal with them. Notice that some of the beggars are men whose limbs are badly deformed or missing: the stump is held out casually before passers-by naked to the seam, like a railroad-crossing bar. Steer wide and shut down, as you've been taught: give no opening. Find it a miserable business and yet older than Job and somehow, in a way you cannot fathom or explain, necessary.

Inevitable Fellows

Rejoice that wine is friendly, inexpensive, ubiquitous. Accept that in most restaurants it is bad, but tolerably so. Exult in window after window of bottles, labels of great beauty displayed like family trophies in chianti shops and *salumeria*, tableaux of salamis and mountains of cheeses and flatbreads, fresh focaccia and calzone. Celebrate wine's brethren: handmade pasta. Pillows and *sombreri* of ravioli stuffed with carciofi, pecorino, *pera*. Pestos of brilliant green, but also red. Locate beer, frizzante and prosecco, cold and diverse and cheap, in the tiniest *alimentari*. Until you graduate to grappa or hard spirits, find nothing offering a high alcohol percentage.

Grasp early that Italians are seldom seen publicly drunk.

That would be *brutta figura*.

Decide all this (exempting the bad wine) to be the blueprint for excellent life—until you are hungover.

Notice then, however, that even hangovers here feel less onerous than elsewhere. Notice that with the passage of hours, *the hangover begins to cure itself*.

Weigh the possibility that many Italians view the whole of life exactly this way.

Shop Windows

Wonder why shops are usually closed, their contents mysterious as Mary Poppins's rounds. Itemize what you see: dusty, crumbling books, violins and mandolins, vases and dishes, forged bells, paintings from centuries-old flea markets, maps, inscrutable scientific instruments, decrepit birdcages, flags, buttons, globes, chess sets, rusting anchors, pulp paperbacks in multiple languages, bedframes, empty bottles, belts, sconces, trays, mirrors, cracked pages from old botanical texts of hand-tinted prints torn out and framed. Etchings and woodcuts. Bad art. Bad furniture. Exquisite art. Exquisite furniture, draped with insanely expensive tapestries. Chandelier crystals. Kitchen appliances. Living room sets. Faience. Crates of tarnished, unmatched jewelry. Gilt sculpture. Murano glass. Religious icons. Life-sized statuary. Broken toys, cheesecake photos, unclassifiable *objets* from the 1950s. Wooden clocks painted in garish designs, pendulums ticking away.

Fail to understand how the owners of these shops keep the businesses going. Reason that the property must have stayed in the owner's family for generations; whatever powers that could close it (if they wished) have been paid off.

Recall that this is how things roll here, though few speak of it.

The National Mystery

Marvel that almost no one in Italy owns a clothes dryer. Tell yourself you feel comforted by the sight of laundry flying like the national flag on pullied lines outside windows. Learn that wet clothes, during winter, must be draped on radiators and little freestanding Tinkertoy contraptions inside every building. At first fancy this charming, *La Vie de Bohème.* Soon find it a supersonic pain in the ass. Note that things take three, four, five days to dry— sometimes never—that towels grow mildewed; window glass sticky with steam; mosquitoes bloated and whirring at your ear all night.

Watch mold blossom across walls.

Coffee

Size up the formal options: espresso from a thimble (tossed back like a tequila shot) or a munchkin cup of Americano (espresso with hot water) or cappuccino (hot milk added). Nescafe machines in hotel lobbies produce a muddy, bitter liquid. Know beforehand that Starbucks maintains no presence in Italy. Remember an online statement from Starbucks's founder, ruffly with romantic arabesques, about not wishing to interfere with the glory of Italian coffee traditions. Feel amused that Starbucks suffers no second thoughts about interfering with the glory of French or Spanish or Irish or German coffee traditions.

Understand that Starbucks refuses (at this writing) to pay off Italian gatekeepers. Suspect that the pressure, from both sides, is building.

First, Wash the Glass

Summon the rental agency rep to solve several problems: patches of fuzzy blue mold snaking across several walls. The oven does not work. One-third of the sliding plastic shower door panels repeatedly falls off. Several lightbulbs have died.

Greet the husband of the agency proprietor, Alberto. He is gentle and courtly, fair-skinned, salt and pepper crew cut, sweater and jeans, modest build. An Italian Fred Rogers: soft, attentive, his English better than your Italian. He shows you how to work the dials to activate the oven. He peers into the oven's maw, which of course you have not yet touched.

Then he faces you and says evenly: But before you can use the oven you must *clean it first*. And you must clean it *very well*, so no soap will burn.

Stare at him. After a moment, gently explain that it's your understanding that everything in a rented place will be clean and ready to use upon arrival.

Watch Alberto's face drain and fall: an expression of gravity and deepest sadness.

You have made a brutta figura. Alberto tries to clarify to the benighted foreigner.

Here in Florence, he begins, with visibly mustered patience, it's never certain how well a *previous tenant* will clean. His face brightens with an illustrative example. If I, Alberto, come to a new place, and I want a glass of water—here he pauses, watching you carefully—First, I *wash the glass.*

Stare, alongside your husband, at Alberto. By telepathic agreement, choose to say nothing. How can you destroy the *bella figura* Alberto is giving his heart in attempting to make?

Alberto asks you to pay for the replacement lightbulbs.

In a spasm of largesse, he buys you a can of oven cleaner and sponges.

Put them under the sink.

Take them out later to paw at the fuzzy blue mold.

Behind the Spectacle

Conclude that the late Luigi Barzini, in his incomparable study *The Italians*, is the only writer who correctly explains Italian culture and character.

Recognize—through Barzini—that Italians are a sad, embattled lot with an excruciating history. The Church, past wars, a series of disastrous governments, and The Family, followed by organized crime, have ruled them forever. The need to create a bella figura, a beautiful spectacle or show to console, distract, and entertain, works to a degree (and initially dazzles the visitor).

Recognize that behind the glittery curtain lurks a labyrinth of punishing corruption, want, resignation, pork-barreling, favoritism. Those who work are bled by taxes and by religious and mob-related tithing; the rest savor obscene, buffered wealth.

See it in the exhausted gazes of the market sellers, grocers, concierges, and waitstaff; in the drawn, laconic faces of clerks and docents; the very elderly being walked by their grown children on Sundays; the grown children themselves; tellers in train station windows.

Life is fuckin' hard here, yells one black man selling worthless packets of tissue in the Mercato di Sant'Ambrogio, where the fabulous meats, cheeses, fish, pestos, breads, desserts, and limitless delicacies are also sold.

Remind yourself of what a local friend declared—that all Italians talk about is when Germany will step in to run things.

Murmur to yourself, vaguely ashamed: *But the pleasures are real.*

Answer yourself at once: *Only if you can pay for them.*

Crave Barzini's voice like that of a trusted, tired, wise but hapless father. Be struck by how, above all, Barzini is very sad.

Admire that Barzini does not apologize for his countrymen. He loves them. He grieves for them. He will not cover for them.

. . . and it is this feeling of being trapped within the inflexible limits of national inclinations which gives Italian life, under the brilliant and vivacious surface, its fundamentally bitter, disenchanted, melancholic quality.

Admit that however confounding, there is palpable charm in Barzini's fatalism—and in that of almost everyone here.

Upon finishing this superb yet mercurial book, realize that you cannot clearly describe it to yourself or to anybody else.

Start the book again the moment you finish it.

Reprise the Domestic

Alberto has managed to install a cable box that he assures you will allow your husband to watch soccer. Pay Alberto the requested fifty euros for this service. Thank him elaborately.

Feel amazed as he seizes your hand and kisses it.

Feel less amazed when no soccer appears the first time your husband tries it. The television screen requests special payment to an 800 number.

Feel still less amazed when one February night, the hot water and heat stop. Touch the radiators in the freezing morning: corpse-cold. Take icy showers, howling, in a frigid apartment. Climb into long johns and send emergency email to the agency.

Read the agency owner's apology: the problem "must be the

boiler." Assume she means the mini–water heater, what the British call a geezer, in a small utility closet. Hope that someone other than Alberto will come.

Alberto arrives.

Stand at the open door as he strides past you declaring *it is two minutes to fix, very simple.* Wait while he goes into the closet and twists a couple of knobs. Slowly, the water warms.

Thank Alberto. Ask whether the problem is your fault, whether you yourself can fix it. Feel slightly vindicated when Alberto tells you the problem is not your fault. Feel unreassured when he says it is too dangerous for you to handle, that he is almost sure it will not happen again for the rest of your stay—

But that it might.

But he lives nearby, he adds cheerfully, and can therefore always come fix it.

Alberto takes your icy hands. He pantomimes blowing on them to warm them, and grins.

He asks, still smiling and holding your hands, whether your husband is enjoying the television soccer.

Neighbors

One morning after you step from the shower, discern a sound like the droning of a bee swarm from the air vent.

Listen carefully. The sound also resembles the song of a Native American war dance, taking quick inhalations and droning on with a little push of intensity.

Someone above you is chanting. Many someones, in never-ending rounds.

Your neighbors seem mainly to be old Italian women who pant as they labor up and down the stairs. But just once, on the stairs, you glimpsed a small, slender Asian man of early middle age.

Decide he is the chanter. Maybe the other voices are recorded. At least the chanter does not pursue his passion late at night. (He does pursue it early some mornings.) Feel assuaged that no bee swarm lives in the walls. Reflect that the chanting may somehow act in an anodyne way, help detoxify the building, the city, the world.

Wonder what the chanter does with his life when he is not chanting. Whom or what does the chanter love, besides the Buddha, or the infinite chain of being? Has he renounced conventional pastimes?

Assume that his is one of the million screened-off stories of Firenze, like the courtyards hidden away off the street that you only glimpse as someone is shutting the tall wooden door upon them while you pass.

Italian logic

The dishwasher has broken. It's a very old model. You've used it just twice, in strict accordance with Alberto's instruction.

Alberto arrives to explain that the agency must *charge you* to repair the machine.

Feel your stomach drop. Try again to explain your understanding of rental agreements. *No no.* Alberto holds up his hands. It does not work that way here. Here in Italy, he says, it is as if *the tenant owns the building.*

After surges of discussion at accelerating volume, feel quasi-relief that the agency agrees to share the repair bill with you. Watch the old dishwasher be removed by workmen. Have no faith that you will see it again. The kitchen floor is covered with water.

Alberto wags a finger at you before he leaves, winking.

You are very lucky, he says.

Eternity in a Teacup

Review the places you have walked in silent awe: the bridges, towers, cathedrals and quilted countryside, ageless hilltop retreats whose names surge in and out of existence.

Stand at the highest lookout point from the Boboli Gardens, red-roofed splendor flung in all directions, olive groves, cypress, castles on the horizon.

Read *Brunelleschi's Dome*. Feel unbearably moved by what it took to build the great jewel at the city's heart.

Walk again through the Bargello, the Uffizi, the Accademia, the Strozzi. Stand before Botticelli, Masacchio, Caravaggio—before the David, white god, testament of infinite tenderness. Walk around him. Pinch back tears. Notice that the pupils of the David's eyes are small holes carved in the shape of plump hearts.

Wander into churches filled with frescoes whose colors seem washed by dreams, into the perfect, small coliseum at Fiesole.

Think, *my eyes saw this*.

Remind yourself how quickly mortal eyes come and go.

Feel time expand and collapse, like lungs.

In the Stone Streets

Give coins to the saxophonist, the cellist, the Django Reinhardt–style jazz trio. Wonder how these artists eat. Crave the music like food. Marvel at such sound in stone quarters where other, ancient, unspeakable things played out.

The Basta Moment

As days give over, still rain-drenched and cold well into April—crowds in the streets growing larger, longer, rowdier—be unable to ignore the creeping inversion.

After Rome, Venice, Sorrento, Assisi, Perugia, Siena, San Gimignano, Bologna—realize there's a template for city and town.

And with it, inescapably, a queer desolation. A sense of entrapment.

Reflect: there is always, in setting out, the dream of the thing. In time, there is but the thing itself. Two worlds.

David Leavitt, in *Florence: A Delicate Case*, got it right. Generations of Forsterian pilgrims—the young Forster himself—sought "to satisfy in Florence some elusive idea of personal fulfillment with which the city's reputation has always been bound up."

But ultimately, Leavitt observes, that "mirage of fulfillment . . . retreat[s] into the distance, and the paradise of exiles reveal[s] itself for what it really [is]: the most elegant, interesting and comfortable of prisons."

Allow that this must surely prove true elsewhere—and yet—

Consider that what had at first seemed the perfect scale for a city now feels cramped and lurid, smelling of Nutella and sugary fried foods, as though you've been camping in the middle of a circus or state fair. Feel sad that more and more Fiorentinos must live elsewhere, renting or selling their homes and apartments to foreign visitors. Sadly agree with local comparisons of Firenze to the city of Venice, which is no longer a civic community but purely, irreparably, a theme park. Employees flee at closing time. Understand you're part of the reason for this. Understand with more sadness that the alternative—desertion, fundlessness, ruin—is no more commendable.

Notice that the Arno is filthy. Plastic bags and other debris catch and eddy along its banks. Feel drained by stone; by hordes of gabbling tourists jamming every passageway while stuffing food into their mouths; by the repeating jewelry and scarves and chocolate and leather bags and restaurant menus like a looping film scrim. Feel suddenly inured to doorways filled with salamis and cheeses and bottles of chianti, to false pleasantries with salespeople. Feel no kinship with the fact that fifty thousand scholars inhabit the city at any given moment. Care little to know that if you spit, you'll hit an art historian or someone who speaks four languages. Wish never to hear another whining Vespa or see another forbearing Madonna or mortified Christ. Feel little guilt about this. Long for Indian or Chinese or Mexican food. Long for good water pressure; for stark, dry horizons; for mesquite and eucalyptus.

Feel sullen, restless. Spend too much time online. Drink too much coffee. Stalk from room to room aligning objects. Feel unappeased, inchoate.

Start to think you hear the chanters, sotto voce, day and night.

Give no spare change to street musicians anymore. Their excellence makes it worse. Storm past them without looking.

Make lists on slips of paper. *Sweep. Laundry. Toilet paper. Drano. Cookies/whatever.* Stuff the papers in your pockets. Lose them.

Drink too much wine.

Commence round after round of push-ups and sit-ups each morning. Stare out at the Arno afterward, breathing hard.

Start recognizing waiters and hostesses from trattorias where you've eaten as they pass you on the street. They are thin, smoking, hurrying away: furtive and spent like actors who've dropped character, hastening from the stage. Wish you hadn't seen this.

Announce yourself sick unto death of draping clothing and towels and linens over radiators and furniture for days on end. Despise the useless radiators. Start to pay four euros per half hour for dryers at the tiny laundromat around the corner. Lug giant sacks of clothing and bedding to-and-fro, cursing as clean underwear falls to the street.

Fret that Alberto's agency will charge you for the gummy shower door propped against the wall, for the blue mold, the uncleaned oven. Hate it when the mosquito you smash bursts with fresh red blood. Fester over the fact that Italian detergents don't seem to understand their purpose, consisting mainly of perfume. Clean the bathroom with Maestro Lindo and note that the room smells like 1952 department store cologne.

Develop terrible trouble sleeping. Have nightmares. Wake sweating at 3:00 a.m., fanning off the mosquito at your ear. Feel alarm at how your heart pounds. Blame the wine. Find yourself unable to stop thinking of everyone you've ever known and everything that ever happened. Stand at the window at dawn and look at the glittering water, the thousand-year-old San Niccolo tower.

Toss and toss in bed, like a fast-forward film. Give up at

6:00 a.m. Go to the computer and stare at American life: its big cars and big bodies; its white teeth, braying slogans and bromides, backward baseball caps and flip-flops; its relentless, hypercaffeinated cheer.

Get into the shower as the church bells start.

Feel unmoved by the bells. Sense that the bells now mock you.

Notice the blue mold has sprung back twice as prolific in the kitchen like a merry pox, blooming exactly where you'd cleaned as if nourished by the cleaning fluid.

A Time to Every Purpose

Commence, at last, the countdown to leaving.

Feel complicatedly relieved. Start packing early. Miss— vulgarly—your gym; fresh, dry clothing; objects on familiar shelves. Miss wide streets, modern art, barbecue and gigantic salads, craft beer, the library, swimming, rented movies, cheap drugstores, autonomy, a decent sleep, late summer nights, crickets, pine-spiced air of redwoods, dry golden hills.

The sharp, saline smell of the northern California sea.

Miss American English.

Miss a round, rising sense of possibility.

Recall that it was exactly this quality you'd vowed to nurture in Italy.

Feel ashamed.

Recall Shirley Hazzard's words.

One needs leisure; one needs imagination. And something more: vulnerability.

Re-pledge allegiance to those words, and to Henry James's injunction—to be someone on whom nothing is lost.

Understand you will continue to fail spectacularly at this.

Resolve it anyway.

Wake in mid-April, with no prelude, to a hot sun in a clear sky.

See the city fan out in light: ochre, salmon, cream, pink marble, surfaces dusted with gold.

Feel your face open. Recollect Keats's maxim, that beauty is truth.

One truth, anyway.

Truth enough.

Wade into the streets. The wind is soft. Breathe beneath the sun.

Try to get lost.

A Bag of One's Own

You might not be able to tell just by looking. Harmless lady, you might suppose—if you bothered to suppose anything.

In fact? The lady is a freak, a fetishist. An addict and a user. Sweating and chafing inside. Struggling to cling to the wagon—careening at that wagon's edge, arms windmilling and flapping like a compressed-air dummy, fighting not to tumble off.

I dream about luggage. Handbags. Backpacks. Duffels. Book bags, messenger bags, beach totes. Two- and four-wheelers. Theft-proof, slash-proof. Secret compartments, hooks for detachable straps or change purses or keyrings. And those mesh cubes you zip in two places to squish their contents flatter, thereby, in theory, creating more room in your case, where the cubes are pictured as fitting with military precision like sleek internal organs.

Even *thinking* about them punches up my pulse. I turn to gawk, without shame, at the bags people carry. I pore over magazine pages, stop in front of shop windows to assess the array in a hungry sweep. Verdicts range: *hopelessly expensive, hopelessly heavy, hopelessly fashion-bound, intriguing, seductive, wait maybe that's the one, maybe that's really the one I've needed all this time, no no no walk away this minute and do not, do not, look back.* I visit certain items online for weeks, even months at a time, studying the products from every angle—debating merits, second-guessing drawbacks, rereading reviews from citizens who can't always spell or articulate too good—before (trembling, heart pounding) pressing the "check out with PayPal" button.

Then, counting the days, I wait—in an agony of self-doubt—for my choice to arrive, when I will be confronted with the hard results of my mad-scientist foamings and schemings. Was my hunch correct, or did I screw up?

When the product arrives I tell myself, against a softly crumbling excitement, that I was correct; oh-ho, this will solve everything. It will be excellent. If it's smaller than expected, I tell myself it will force me to streamline. Then, like any new thing, it begins to leak excellence. Streamlining starts to feel like wearing shoes that are too tight. After a couple of months I find myself drawn, sickened and drawn, mothlike (by enticing ads in the margins of the work I'm supposed to be doing) to the e-Bags page once again.

How did this happen? What can it mean?

As a young woman, I didn't care *that* way. A bookish, melancholic, hormonal adolescent, I carried my stuff in anything. I recall liking totes—reasonable enough, given a student's loads of books. But I honestly can't remember any carrier itself mattering almost *morally*, the way it matters now. As a young woman (before the Internet) I found purses and luggage at bargain shops, outmoded lines offered cheaply for quick sale, easily (and nonchalantly) replaced when they fell apart. I don't remember angsting. Certainly I never obsessed the way I now obsess—shamefully. Metabolism-changingly.

But I can trace the sprouting of the seed. And I can connect the urge (the pathology, if you wish) to something nobler.

A subtle, graduated progression, but distinct.

I am guessing the first symptoms germinated—stay with me—in an early fascination with *the ways things fit*. Objects in boundaried spaces. *The relationships of objects to their containment.* A cubbyhole's contents—a jacket, some books, a favorite toy, neatly stored—charmed and disarmed. It was like a little house, perfectly sized for its inhabitants.

I recall my sharp pleasure, as a toddler, eyeballing that cozy snugness—along with a slow-breaking awareness: things could be sheltered *while* being given adequate breathing space.

This combination, I thought without words, respected the unique thingness of things.

Did Joseph Cornell start this way?

That satisfaction did something to the mind, some tectonic shift you could feel. It induced a vision—a Platonic ideal—of order and repose, alongside access and readiness. Things calmly rested in their designated space until you needed them. They stood at attention, easy-to-hand. Their peaceful coexistence gave relief to the perceiving human, even a still-quite-small human. I'm uncertain why, or how, it works. (Fêng shui experts will surely be glad to explain.) But the effect is as real now as it was then—like burying one's face in fresh flowers.

Now take this understanding to the next, entrancing step: lunchboxes.

With lunchboxes—crucially—the child's mind meets the same principles of order and repose, but wrapped in a new notion: *portability*.

What might portability mean to a child? Ah. Think of fairy tales, mythology, the Bible. The most ancient, most common, most popular story ever told: *someone goes on a journey*. Children, never least, went on journeys with delicious regularity in oft-told tales. Hansel and Gretel. The Darling siblings, the Boxcar children. Pinocchio, Oliver Twist, and David Copperfield. Huck Finn; later, Holden Caulfield. (In the well-loved Signet paperback cover illustration of *Catcher in the Rye*, you may recall, we see Holden from behind. Notable, besides the red baseball cap—backward—is that he's clutching an old-fashioned, bourbon-brown leather suitcase, a couple of university stickers glued onto it. Oh, that dull glow; that burnished leather. Heaven help me.)

The list has no end. Kids lit out for the territories, the great cities, blue yonder, Neverland, the high seas, *Into the Woods*. No one knew what would happen, least of all the pint-sized wayfarers. Listen to Paul Theroux's first sentences in his preface to *The Tao of Travel*: "As a child, yearning to leave home and go far away, the image in my mind was of flight—my little self hurrying off alone

. . . to find a new self in a distant place, and new things to care about."

The old term for it, seldom used anymore, is "seeking one's fortune." And fortune did not so much then mean money, strangely, as it meant future adventure; or, in Grace Paley's famous words, the "open destiny of life." Brave children in legend and folklore left home, knapsack or rucksack or buckskin pouch or knotted-up tablecloth slung over a thin shoulder or narrow back. (Two classics thrilled me when I was very young, accounts of resourceful orphans exiled into the countryside: *Nobody's Boy* and *Nobody's Girl*—translated from the French *Sans Famille*—by Hector Malot. Oh, the genius of these little explorers' foragings, their inventions for food and shelter! Oh, to sleep on a bed of ferns, to eat watercress soup and wild berries!)

Remember, irony had no place in dreams back then. And those dreams shaped grown-up visions of more than mere travel. They shaped the way we consider the full trajectory of our lives—the open destiny of every breaking day. (Cue our modern fondness for the word *journey* as a synonym for experience.) Each of us—even the most bitterly calcified, the most stuck, the most sealed-off—is technically a pilgrim, if only by virtue of living through a span of linear time in specific ways.

Thus, we return to the *satchels* (the word like caramel between the teeth).

Satchels contained, naturally, the adventurers' most necessary possessions—*the stuff they needed in order to keep being who they were* in the vast unknown. A child identifies in an eyeblink with such stories. They become *her* stories. (Imagined and real are fluid categories, two rivers feeding each other.) Along with clothing or shoes, in these stories children brought objects that comforted: a stick or stone, a leaf, a tooth. Possessions were pieces of her, the familiar tugged into the unfamiliar: therefore protection. Therefore magic.

By extension, the thing that contained *and* hefted those objects along likewise had magic.

I remember the just-rightness with which a thermos, a sandwich, an apple, a cookie, and maybe a little bag of chips, dovetailed inside my lunchbox. The sight—clean symmetry, crisp Mondrian rectangularness—soothed. (Never mind most lunchboxes also smelled of old bologna or peanut butter. Many have been comforted by that smell.) You stared at the filled box with the same pleasure you felt running a hand over the smoothly interlocked seams of a finished puzzle. Then you clicked shut the lid (that thick, smart *snap*), grasped the lunchbox by its perfectly fitting handle. And off you went, swinging your carrying arm for the joy of it, toting your snug little conglomerate of food, art, and self. (Even a brown-bag lunch wafted some twinkling, if crumpled, specialness.)

Setting forth, you felt fortified. Invigorated as much by the *knowledge* of provisions as by the fact of them; goodies borne by your own strength. This understanding, in turn, prompted a sense of self-sufficiency—a wakening awareness of Self's relationship to World.

Lunchboxes mattered.

Their design and color (though my kid brain couldn't consciously say so) emblemized identity like a personal crest or flag. Here began a sense of autonomy, of agency. The way the lunchbox looked had to make a true statement about you. Never mind Disney logos, Barbie motifs, superheroes. My favorite box, for a long time, bore a rich, red tartan plaid.

Now skip forward to high school graduation. What sings out?

A typewriter case.

It cheers me just to picture it.

My beloved, late dad, a college teacher, gave me his own Royal Portable as a graduation gift. A compact, dark gray machine—considered sporty for its day—cool to the touch with shiny, dark-green keys. I cherished the machine-oil-and-ribbon-ink smell of it. Never mind it had been well used by my Pop. It worked fine, made superb music when the typing got going, and I couldn't have been happier. It meant as much as a car—maybe more. It would be my ticket into the *open destiny of life*. I would evoke that destiny by typing it. The typewriter was a time machine, a transmogrifier like that of Calvin and Hobbes, a Sword in the Stone—proof of bona fides.

Its carrying case, in truth, was awkward: pillow shaped, exterior a bumpy-textured tweed. But on the case's interior (mauve, smooth, spacious) I scotch-taped scraps of paper upon which I'd typed inspiring quotes and aphorisms. The quotes seemed wise and important; they gave me heart. J. D. Salinger was among those quoted, or rather some of his characters—Holden, the grown Glass children. Others: maybe Krishnamurti, Kahlil Gibran, Herman Hesse. Maybe Lillian Hellman, Mary McCarthy, Isaac Dinesen, Katherine Anne Porter, Carson McCullers. I had crushes on all of them, and many more, at different intervals. Maybe I was an arrogant ninny. But a growing mind needs a push, and over a bridge of years it falls to some gauzy combination of instinct and imagination to help do the pushing.

Case and contents, then, promised sparkling possibilities. That is, they would wick those possibilities from me and feed them along, like oil from a lamp to feed its flame. My father had deputized me. I could enter the world armed (by this larger lunchbox) and anointed. I was pretty sure, in some deep chamber of churning urgency, that everything to come, everything I would encounter, would feed art-to-come. I never thought it in those words, but I was fairly vibrating with the conviction. (Ultimately it *did* happen exactly that way, though it took a hella long time. Thank you again, Daddy. I love and miss you.)

The typewriter case, then, was the gateway drug.

Now, fast-forward the analog clock again. When did things get serial-wacko between me and luggage? How did bags become something more, something libidinous, something Other?

That rabbit hole gaped open, I think, after I met the man I would later marry. He was a teacher, and every few years he taught a semester abroad. I traveled with him: Paris more than once, Florence. Because the distance (not to mention expense) to Europe from California's Bay Area is considerable, he was eager to cram in as much as we could, adding on an extra month of wandering after each teaching obligation ended. On different trips we visited Greece and Turkey, Germany and Spain, Croatia, Prague, Sicily. And because he is from England and has family and friends there, plenty of stopovers happened there, too.

With those years came the first tough packing challenge: climate. Sometimes we stayed through a winter into part of a summer. That meant checking a big suitcase full of winter clothing on the flight over, hauling it to wherever we'd be living, storing it (full of winter stuff) when we left the host city as weather warmed, then collecting the monster from storage after wanderings were done (in serious heat), and finally towing it back to the airport for checking on our return home. In a word: *ordeal.* I can't forget dragging a case the size of a pony through the streets of Florence, in blazing heat. Its wheels did not function right, so it limped and listed and wobbled as I swore and sweated and hated everything.

(Cab drivers were striking that day. Transport strikes in Europe are constant as bread; cabbies take turns, as if in some scripted dance, with bus drivers, airlines, subways, trains.)

Certainly, I always overpacked. That remains a given, perhaps gender-mandated (though I'm a passionate feminist). Or it may be a residual reflex from some primal, cultural mandate (meaning Jewish, meaning what's sewn into your coat lining on the escape boat is what you'll be living on, or bartering with, in the New World). These are both minefield subjects, and I wouldn't want to speak for others. But I admit to an overpowering need to feel that I have stashed what may be wanted—if only a couple of tissues to sneeze into—and to know what is where, at any given time. Why else does my husband begin so many queries to me with *Do we have . . .* and *Where are the . . . ?*

My husband, by contrast, owned so little during the first half of his life it never occurred to him to pack a lot thereafter. He's a minimalist—something I admire. He hates what he calls "fussing." Plus, he's a man. He can wear the same things all the time and nobody cares; he never needs makeup or female products. He'll wash with anything or not at all; sad to say, I've sometimes had to remind him. I am certain that on a moment's notice my wonderful mate would gladly lope out the door with just a toothbrush in his hand—that in fact if I, the Hygiene Sheriff, did not insist upon it, he might not bother grabbing that.

I can only sigh. I need toiletries. I need choices. And I need to feel prepared.

I have risen from bed in the middle of the night to repack, lying to myself that this was the final round of it.

My fixation accrued, I think, during those Long Crossings with him. Several of them, to-and-fro, taught me something both fundamental and monumental:

What you took, and the way you took it, figured hugely in the experience—and in your memory of it.

As years progressed I began to discern patterns—many of joy, others of pain and frustration. Repetitions forced me (facing prospects of much more voyaging) to square off with the unthinkable:

How can I get a grip on this? How can a woman truly simplify, in transit?

How to get back the dream—the plucky rover tramping out to meet the world, swinging along her delightful (and not heavy) lunchbox?

Slowly, a grading system took shape. You had to boil down to the grittiest (and in any other context, the silliest) details. On the road, they counted. Everything counted.

Fair warning: we now enter the portals of fetishism. Feel free to turn back.

I saw that there was no sense, for starters, using a carry-on case that weighed over five pounds. Five pounds, before you toss in a comb, is a lot of weight. (You'd be amazed how many products out there, hyped as ultralight, actually weigh a ton. More astoundingly, for a long while luggage makers *did not even list* weights. Criminal.)

I also began to think like a physicist about what features of Things Carried and Carrier Itself had become nonnegotiable.

There are trade-offs. Weighing them (no pun), one keeps having to start from scratch.

"Scratch" means asking again and again: *What is absolutely necessary, and how can I get my hands on it fast and easily?*

You learn—you invent—en route. So after what might be politely termed a long, *long* trial period—stubbornly believing there exists out in the bagosphere one design that embodies the *perfect answer*, which of course is never true—I have a muscle-memory sense of what works.

Here, for example, is what I've learned about handbags.

For some time I thought a small backpacky thing served as the best handbag because it freed one's arms and hands. *Wrong. So wrong.* It means that every single time you need a coin or pen or scarf you must remove the accursed packy thing from your back, zip it open, seize your item, zip it closed, wriggle it back on. Those actions, repeated thousands of times, make you nuts. (Bonus suffering points if the straps keep slipping off your shoulders and you have to tie them with a scarf or bungee cord across your chest to keep them on, so that you appear to be wearing a sort of lederhosen.) Your husband is steamed at having to stop and wait every time you perform these actions, especially on crowded streets or turnstiles in subways with thousands of humans pouring around you or pressing at your backs.

Also, he doesn't like the lederhosen effect.

(What do men do? They take one small carry-on; keep wallet and passport in the belt gizmo around their middles. That's *it*. Admirable, yes. Feasible for me, no.)

The female traveler learns, the excruciating way, that a handbag works best worn lightly across the front of the body at an instantly reachable angle—*worn at all times*, even sitting down. None of us is incapable of leaving the cleverest, most theft-proof bag on a hook beside a train seat, for example, so that said bag continues to travel by itself all the way to Venice and back, after which some saintly soul turns it in at the Florence train station lost-and-found, which then emails you to come and claim the bag—thank God you left a card in it with your email address printed on it—though the lost-and-found-master turns out to be busy chatting with colleagues and drinking coffee and can't be bothered to notice that you have arrived to claim your bag and are waiting there, let alone that your bag is right *at his feet* when he finally, drawlingly asks you—after standing there all that time, waiting—to describe the bag.

That's why the term *cross-body* becomes extra meaningful in online shopping.

Finally: the bag must open and close fast and easily, so that at a glance you can see and touch everything inside and grasp what's wanted in a nanosecond, even while walking. Even while running.

The trade-off? Size. You can't fit a book or a bottle into it. (This is probably good: less impulse buying.) Your husband can't ask you to stash his own detritus. Suggest he carry his own bag. (Brace yourself for resentment shrapnel.)

Now apply similar motives to a (super-lightweight) carry-on: supremely difficult. If your belongings feel like extensions of yourself and therefore magically protect you from the chaotic world, this makes it very, very tough to cast stuff aside. It makes you feel naked and vulnerable, like a shell-less turtle. You have to smack your memory hard, over and over, to remind it how those very same items, once in transit, truly do become stinking albatrosses around your neck, heavy clutter that adds pain. Remember the *exact details* of staring at the unused clothes or shoes (what country, what room, what time of day) while thinking, clearly and bitterly: *I should never have brought these.*

For a stab at discipline, try packing once, letting it sit a day, then ripping the case apart and packing half as much, keeping the above fierce memory front and center.

Then wait another day. Do it again. Lose a little more. In an emergency you can buy stuff.

(There are three items of clothing—a friend claims sadly—that you wind up using through an entire trip. The problem? You can't know what they are until you're there.)

Now comes the confession, probably self-evident, saved up to blurt just here: I fail.

I fail myself and my husband and the whole damned enterprise, without letup. I fail and fail and fail. I use a small, lightweight carry-on and a sleek tote containing a compact handbag for later use, once belongings are dumped in a room. But no matter how I strive to cut away, cut back, cut down, I wind up overstuffing these, so they're awkward and painful to drag around. I feel stupid and foolish. No bag on earth has yet cured or solved this. I keep believing I will get it right the next trip. I fail again.

(Reading Paul Theroux gives a bit of comfort. In *The Tao of Travel* he lists what famous travelers have hauled with them, across the generations. Many needed caravans of porters. Also, some, like the late Bruce Chatwin, apparently lied, and took far more than they admitted to.)

But, see, I can't lose the shining ideal: *travel light.*

It's like a song you can't scrub from your head. It goes with the gear. The gear *evokes* it. Like advertising, the gear creates the need.

But let's say, larkily, that you and I have held to the leanest laws and managed it: unpacked, dumped, repacked at half the weight. Let's say we've at last, in blissful theory, forged a workable balance. *Now* we can be that guy in the old woodcut illustration, sticking his head through the seam at the horizon, gazing in wonder at the dazzling cosmic watchworks. We're deft, simple, canny. We can step out of a train or plane or boat or bus with an easy gait, an open, relaxed face (and mind and heart): modest valise in hand, distilled-to-featherweight handbag across chest. We can concentrate with alert compassion on what's around us—what any of it may or may not mean—and on our own grains-of-sand part in the infinite mystery of creation.

And bag addiction need not throw shade on this mission, right?

Rationally, I understand. Bags are not the mystery. *I* am the mystery. Except with precedents scrolling back—as we have seen—to childhood, the gear is intimately *bound up with* the mystery. Bag fetishism, I politely swear, posits Ways to Enter the World, backlit by those timeless children's stories and their adult ripening, the spirit of the pilgrim soul.

(Google the brilliant cartoon by Richard Stine, called *Romantic Enters the World*. It shows a gaga-faced young man wearing a pointy dunce cap, a sickly half smile on his lips and a single rose in his hand, stepping glassy-eyed off a cliff: below wait a pack of gleeful wolf creatures whose opened jaws bear rows of razor teeth.)

Nothing's simple.

But resolve doesn't cost anything.

So we can resolve—again and again—to be the flâneur, loosed in the maze of the shining capital, the vagabond minstrel striding the meadow, singing while cowbells echo from a distant ridge. *I love to go a-wandering, along the mountain track, and as I go, I love to sing, my knapsack on my back.*

At the starting line of it all, modeled by red plaid lunchboxes and bulky typewriter cases—was this not the original vision?

Nonetheless, I can't help myself. I must wonder:

What *kind* of knapsack?

Cave of the Iron Door

- - - - - - - - - - - - - - - - - - -

> "What I wanted to say . . . was: *I could not bear it,*
> but out of my mouth came the words, 'I cannot bear it.'"
>
> —WILLIAM MAXWELL, *SO LONG, SEE YOU TOMORROW*

The surface couldn't have looked simpler. A brief getaway, some extra warmth at a chilly time of year. On the face of it, so natural. A visit to your old hometown—your *first* hometown, *pays natal*, place of birth, original setting for those big-bang memories. People smiled and nodded when you told them. Wholesome as a Fourth of July picnic. Yet I remember my heart squeezing as the plane touched asphalt, white sun deceptively mild through the air-conditioned cabin's window. Out that window: purple-brown desert hills, landscape of childhood. Was it January?

My husband sits beside me on the plane, happily crunching down my ignored mini-bag of mini-pretzels, tapping it to dislodge last bits, his mind dancing (as it does when he sets out anywhere) with images of turquoise swimming pools, tequila cocktails, gritty Mexican food, eye-watering barbecue. He loves heat because he grew up with wrenching cold, so he becomes lavishly cheerful when we're entering a guaranteed-to-bake kingdom. The plane's windows are a pulse of light, like the blur filling Kier Dullea's travel pod in *2001: A Space Odyssey*.

Have I secretly assumed things will stay as I remember them? Maybe everyone who visits her childhood setting, after a lifetime away, has no choice. You have only your own lonely memory to

58

go by. No one else is still alive—no one you know of—to second you, to say *yes, it was that.* What can anyone be sure of, after all? Less and less looks the way it once did.

But tell me—what stays the same in the American West for fifty years? For five?

Sky Harbor Airport: the words still send a shiver. Once the very sound of that name punched us little kids in the chest like the word *Christmas.* Now the image shrinks to that of an old hand-tinted postcard: its single control tower a lone lighthouse, scanning empty expanses of runway in clear, hot sun, its crown a big cut jewel, impenetrable dark glass facets flashing. What dwelt inside? Looming and silent—yes—as the omniscient monolith in *2001.* Takeoffs and landings could in fact have been space launches, as much as their drama dazzled my family.

You went to the airport for thrills: on ultraspecial nights to dinner at Sky Harbor's restaurant, watching planes come and go while you ate. We may as well have been driving our olive drab '49 Ford straight into the future on those evenings: baby sister Andrea and I bouncing along in the back seat (beltless then), dreaming out the windows, singing made-up songs while dust billowed behind the car—so many roads still unpaved. Mesmerized, our family was, pulled as if programmed toward a new modernity: fat propeller planes servicing ant-sized human masters, a shoal of shining silver Airbuses trundling slowly in and out, plump with passengers. Tiny figurine faces smiled through the capsule windows. Tiny figurine hands waved.

Everyone dressed for air travel as if for church, or a dinner party. Men wore fedoras, jackets, ties—sometimes bolo ties. Plenty of cowboy hats, often with business suits for a formal effect. Women wore crisp shirtwaist dresses, or what was heedlessly called a squaw dress: full-skirted, rickrack-and-sequin-trimmed. Petticoats, hose, heels, girdles—gloves and chic hats. Air travel was still viewed as a privilege; Arizona air itself, ultraclear and dry, pre-scribed for sufferers of tuberculosis and joint problems. In that clean light, colors shone true, deep and saturated as stained glass, and the clustered planes threw light back in blinding silver.

From behind a simple chain link fence, easily stepped around—the extent of security—we watched passengers descend like royals, stepping across the tarmac toward us with a kind of self-conscious self-possession. There's something surreal about this (though a child does not yet use that word), about seeing your uncle or grandma step calmly from an enormous silver container—brought *through the sky* from far away—to approach you here on the Arizona tarmac, mere hours later, smiling.

How toylike those components, I think now. How toylike our assumptions.

How toylike most of the creations of men, including rocket ships. Yet in their very thingness—their density, their irreducibility—how brave. How earnestly they'd been fashioned to do their jobs.

For children, these astonishing creations—trains, boats, cars, planes—were monuments to magic. Every part—the rolling staircase, the little rounded cabin door, its deep interior walls cut as if through thick cake like the door into Winnie the Pooh's treehouse—magic. The fat gleaming planes pregnant with miniature people, gentle, tamed creatures doing men's bidding—a giant's pet, a giant's playthings. Through a wall of glass in Sky Harbor's restaurant we could watch the silver creatures lift off and touch down. A pianist played jazz on a white baby grand, stationed atop a central stage. If it was your birthday he played the birthday song while other diners sang along, and the waiters planted a live sparkler on the slice of cake placed before you.

Sparklers.

This isn't the time to look for the restaurant, though.

It's time to locate the rental car station, your husband trailing you, people and luggage pushing past. A normal airport's bustle: white lights, linoleum, loudspeaker noise. But something not normal is also happening. The air feels charged; your body is tensed, half expecting to catch sight of one or more faces from your past floating forward—whirling back to tap you on the shoulder. Excuse me, aren't you—?

Something's begun to pump through your limbs and chest: pulse bearing down. Your body, old animal that it is, recognizes first surfaces, first smells, turning agog toward the dusty lavender mountains (color of an old scar), pebbled flatlands, waxy mesquite, soft yellow Palos Verde petals, red cardinals singing their uncannily sweet song, scent of creosote (like pungent wet metal after it rains). Soon you'll greet favorite cacti: stubby barrel, dignified saguaro, delicate ocotillo, bumpy cholla, prickly pear like needled paddles. Your body has quickened, trembles, alert to this host of living cues. The very air, the purple-brown mountains, their formations, their names: Camelback. Superstition. Praying Monk. Street signs, highways, landmarks: MacDowell. Cave Creek. Indian School Road. Thomas Road. Oak Creek Canyon. The calm desert air. All stand serene, just as they were in your first encounter with them—first map, byways, systems of human community—therefore of meaning—that you ever laid eyes upon, ever took for instruction. Here was the original world. Here was how it had worked.

The floating cosmos, debris still circling in formation. Your big bang.

Time has begun to weave and undulate, to shimmer. It will keep doing this, though you'll give no sign you're falling down a wormhole; no hint that your mind and heart are atomizing, recoagulating, melting and twisting into lava lamp shapes, ballooning open, sucking closed, careening, looping—a murmuration of cells, roused from long sleep.

Outwardly, you're just another aging woman.

Whereas the rental car clerks, my God, are so young.

They could be your grandsons. This your first time in Phoenix? one asks. Here on business? Any good plans? Stuff they're taught to say. Where are these children from? Don't they know they are standing on your home? That you were born in St. Joseph's Hospital and that your dad, a tall handsome wavy-haired Brooklyn native fresh out of Columbia, took the job teaching at Phoenix College and soon helped found Phoenix's Unitarian Church, designed in a then-bold, modernist style, stationed firmly opposite Barry

Goldwater's regal house in the empty desert, giving shelter to left-leaning and liberal thinkers in the aridity of that hyperprovincial, hyperconservative culture? That your dad also worked as a proofreader for the Arizona Republic; that he was hugely charismatic and charming; also hugely promiscuous and maddened by longing for something he could not name that was apparently forever missing? That your mom in her bottomless loneliness during gaping stretches of empty days without him took you and your little sister to hotel pools like the Westward Ho Hotel and the Ramada Inn; bought you curlicue-topped frostees at the Dairy Queen, and when your dad was actually home that you sometimes all went out to eat in restaurants with dark lighting and glittering glass and silver and tinkling ice like Los Olivos, and like Macayo's with its brilliantly colored parrot logo exotic and mysterious (a franchise now), and where your father drank and drank except you didn't know then how much or that there was such a thing as too much; you only made a face at the weirdly ruining bitterness when you tasted his whiskey and Coke or rum and Coke; sweetness of cola so heavenly why would anyone on purpose pour in the gasoline taste? That during other days your mom took you and your baby sis to eat at the Carnation Dairy restaurant where you two little girls sang the Davy Crockett theme together in the women's restroom because the acoustics there were so terrific? That your mom also took you both to eat at Bob's Big Boy where just seeing the towering statue out front, the smiling bulge-bellied boy in checked overalls holding aloft his plated, giant cheeseburger, made you crazy-starved for a cheeseburger and chocolate shake and also for dill pickle slices because when you ate at Bob's (bathed in its blessed air conditioning) you were always given your mom's pickle slices, which if you held them to the light were translucent? That because her days were chasms bigger than the Grand Canyon fillable only by driving her little girls everywhere, she drove you both so many times to fairyland Encanto Park (could any word be lovelier than Encanto?) and you could always tell by the sudden appearance of green grass alongside the highway that Encanto was near and your hearts would start to pound—where you fed the ducks and ran screaming from stretched-neck geese and ate pink, tauntingly sweet cotton candy that melted so fast on your teeth and you paddled the paddle boat on murky algae-smelling lake water and rode the jewel-bright merry-go-round again and again while it played Claire de Lune, the most beautiful song in the history of forever, while from your cresting horses you shouted here I am momma here here hi momma, waving every time your horse passed her and she stood aside smiling tightly behind sunglasses, arms folded in her wool plaid oversized Pendleton shirt, as if always cold? That she also carted you both to the Phoenix Public Library, which resembled a big white-and-pink sheet cake, where again bathed in blissful air conditioning you and your sister ran straight to your favorite sections and checked out piles of books you could hardly carry, especially the biography series of famous women with black silhouettes of their subjects stenciled on the covers like Clara Barton, Florence Nightingale, Louisa May Alcott, Helen Keller?

Couldn't the rental car guys just osmose all that?

Couldn't they sense that you yourself, as a girl, actually somehow managed to be invited to appear on *The Wallace and Ladmo Show*, the local weekday afternoon television kids' show which you and your sister and all the kids in the whole state completely and lovesickly adored the way you also adored *Shock Theater*, which showed hokey old horror films on Saturday mornings hosted by a gruesomely made-up young man called Freddie the Ghoul?

Could they even understand what appearing on Wallace and Ladmo meant?

You only say to these child-men: I was born here.

You stifle the urge to add, hundreds of years ago.

The lads smile blankly as they process paperwork. It must be nice to be so new as to have no thoughts, no tendrils of association, no marks yet left by the world. The car is found. You and your (jolly, unwitting) husband slam yourselves inside it and you, almost panting at the wheel with the intensity of the cosmic onslaught—rippling, pixilated, as if you had swallowed a tab of acid—turn on the air conditioning and creep the car out of the parking lot into a silver-gray afternoon, onto highway surrounded by desert—your desert—which itself, thank the stars, seems not to have changed one bit.

Floaty is how it feels, driving the landscape of earliest memory: set free inside an ancient dream. The desert around you was the first world, the safest world (for a while), the best and only world— best because only. Everything that came afterward, between it and you, seems flimsy—a distraction or occlusion, like swamp fog—all the lives, all the identities grabbed at like slippery buoys since you left this place, age eleven, for California after your mother died of grief, or of what the coroner called an excess of barbiturates in her tiny body, but what you sensed without words through your eleven-year-old bones was a kind of giving up.

It is possible, mused Berna, a friend of your mother and father, that your mother only wanted some sleep.

You, your stunned father, your baby sister, and your dog (in her little carrier) will fly to Sacramento, where your father has already begun a new teaching job.

Confused friends arrive at the Sunnyslope house, blanched with shock, to drink and smoke with your father and listen to him ramble insensibly during your last days there. They ask your father why he is bothering to pack along Ruthie, the gentle, sweet, chestnut-red dachshund you and your little sister so dearly love.

They've lost their mother, your father declares. They'll have their dog.

Your husband reads directions while you drive. (These are the days before cell phones and navigation systems.) Your heart is a nervous rabbit. You glance around—late morning outside clear and parched, already hot, sun glinting off chrome and highway. You're still expecting any second to spot friends from childhood or—siphoning directly from memory—their parents. Or friends of your own dead parents, other founding Unitarians: the Grigsbys, the Michauds, your dad's drinking buddy Dee Filson, his kids, his petite black-haired wife Dottie, on whom he was complicatedly cheating and ultimately divorcing—Dee who nicknamed your wild-ass, tomboy little sister "Vyshinsky," perhaps because the Moscow prosecutor's first name was "Andrei." The dentist Doc Purdyman, his pretty wife Martha. Oscar and Berna Rauch. Gone, gone, gone. Yet you expect to see them, all these familiars, trudging ahead beside your lane on the highway like B-movie zombies, whirling to face you just as your car nears them—to lift a wan hand, flag you down.

Many of your own peers are dead.

You turn up the car's air conditioning.

Something strange has begun, with the writing of this. I am sinking.

The words become a bog, a pudding. I can't urge thoughts forward but only return to pore again and again over initial lines, combing and recombing them. More: I have begun stopping every ten minutes to search online for childhood names—any name—looking for lost beings on social media, prowling high school lists of graduating classes. I find a few immediately. Stare at them, frightened. Still alive. Same name. After my heart somersaults, it freezes. Anxiety and—strangely—shyness fill my chest. Shyness? From a writer immersed for decades in noisy self-promotion, practiced at blasting her own name across social media, buttonholing editors and agents and readers like a carnival pimp to check out her work? Whereas here—in this soupy dream state—my heart shivers, revving in place. Think carefully, it murmurs. Do you really want to puncture your own freedom and privacy, hallooing people who are effectively strangers? What if those names turn out to be people you don't care for? What if, conversely, they're appalled by you? What if, after the first few astonished, titillated sentences, there is nothing left to say? What if they turn out to be unhinged and decide to stalk you?

I found a boy who lived on my street, on whom I'd once had a crush. He's a grandfather now. He sent his photo, photos of his family. Bless the man: he's exactly the same, only old. He is kind and gentle. He understands my need to recover memory, and he sends updates when I ask—cautiously—about names I remember. Loren is simple and forthright:

> *X was a pole-vaulter in high school and did great. He was married and lived in—. Not sure if he had any children. His wife died unexpectedly. He came down a couple of times to visit after his wife had died, when he met up with his high school sweetheart. They married and live in—.*

I tried, several times, to write different individuals. I'd find the address, choose the name, struggle to shape an email. I'd tap out three-quarters of it, kowtowing to soften the shock: *I hope my finding you this way, after all this time, will not upset or disturb you. I live in Northern California now; I'm a novelist—*

Then I'd stop, unable to continue.

I deleted the letters.

Whatever I tell them, what can reasonably follow? What do I truly want from them? What could they truly want from me? What do I imagine can surprise or enlighten either side? They'll have lived lives parallel to mine, falling in love, having children, watching kids grow up and make their own kids. They'll have lost people, logically or not, up and down the hierarchy of age and privilege. They'll have remarried. They'll be widowed, retired. They'll have a cat or dog or cockatiel, goats or weasels or tropical fish. They'll volunteer or play golf, be addicted to crosswords or gardening, television or cheesy mysteries, or be entirely taken up with grandchildren. They'll have a cupboard full of vitamins and meds to swallow nightly, like me; they'll wash dishes in the evening like me, stare into opalescent suds wondering what it can possibly mean to have reached this age. Think of the platoon of us: staring, bewildered, into dish-soap bubbles.

> *Y is married to Z; they had four boys. Y is retired from the sheet metal union as a past union president. They spend summers in—and winters in—.*
>
> *C sells insurance and lived near you. The last time I saw*

him was five years ago and he looked good. He'd married and had a daughter who played volleyball.

Do you remember B? She twirled baton in high school. She had some type of disease and died a few years after we graduated.

One girl I tried to find, a girl with whom I powerfully identified—also deeply envied and admired, a button-nosed strawberry blonde with generous early breasts and a bright, musical voice, someone of whom I'd always felt jealous but with whom I'd spent endless joyful hours at play, dancing, dreaming, eating sleeping laughing swimming—is dead. Laurie Michaud. I was looking online for her when, to my horror, up popped her obituary. She had died three years earlier. No cause was named. No one had alerted me. No one remaining in her life could have remembered my own existence, or how to find me if they had. Laurie had worked as an airline hostess with a then-well-known international company. That made sense; she'd been so effortlessly personable, so beautiful, so sexy. We were the same age. I can still feel the slicing effect of those few small-print obit lines, the unheralded facts of her end, leaking into my body like sand. The obit named a surviving second husband, whom I could not make myself contact. Later I found both her grown sons on Facebook, and one answered politely when I sent a groveling message.

Groveling, yes. Because by what right should I burst into these people's lives, resurrecting the grief they'd surely labored years to control?

Do you remember saying good-bye to us when you had to move away? wrote Loren, the boy on my street who's now a grandfather.

You cried, he wrote, *and said you did not want to go, but that you had to.*

I can remember no such scene. How much else has my child's mind cleanly erased?

Berna told you—some forty years after your mother's death— *there was a moment, during those first few horrible days, when it appeared that your father was considering not keeping you girls.*

She said this haltingly, on the phone, many years ago now, cautioning you first that what she was about to say might shock you.

You remember having trouble taking in her words (though you were listening with furious concentration, hunched at the front desk of your day job, eyes shut tight). You were at that time perhaps thirty-five years old, on a mission to exhume the facts. You'd located Berna by phone and asked her to please tell you whatever she knew. She was willing—eternal credit to that woman—to try. As she spoke you mashed the receiver to your ear, its curly wire tugging at the desk console. You swiveled your desk chair away from passing people, staring out the wide window—the pearl light of afternoon, San Francisco traffic—pressed the receiver harder against your hot ear, plugging the free ear with a finger.

Not keep. Like a hamster that hadn't worked out and needed to be returned to the pet store or donated to a neighbor? Berna, elderly when she spoke those words to you, long dead now—told you she drove straight to your Sunnyslope house after your father, in anguish, phoned her. Berna had been a chic woman: pixie haircut, horn-rim glasses that made her look every bit as smart and droll as she was, a milder Dorothy Parker. Though Berna was pregnant at the time of receiving your father's call and had given up smoking for that reason, she purchased a pack of cigarettes on the way over to your father's house and lit right up when she got there, lighting one also for your father—who'd never stopped smoking and who would only stop when, years later, he became frightened by the angina that had begun to dog him. (The fact that the pills he'd been prescribed indeed eased the angina, he confessed to your sister, frightened him more. He would die of a heart attack thirteen years later, at age fifty-four.)

For days after your mother's death your father held a kind of drunken court, receiving a steady trickle of hapless and horrified friends, colleagues, students. Sitting glazed in the worn nubble of the only easy chair in the house, his customary throne, clutching his whiskey and Coke, he talked and they listened, gathered around him in some modern reenactment of Socrates's final followers, all day and into the night. The kitchen filled up with strange casse-roles left by neighbors. These dishes confused you. Dimly, you sensed that their appearance was part of some primal tradition. But to you they seemed a kind of alien growth, like mushrooms after rain. Jell-O salads, potato salads, macaroni salads.

Berna told you that during those first hours with him she issued the strongest command she had ever uttered, or would ever utter, to your stupefied father.

Bob, she said, *on no terms, under no circumstances, must you ever again entertain the idea of not keeping those girls.*

Not only, during this Return of the Native, will you see no famil-iar face: nothing glamorous will be visible for the duration of the journey. The city of Phoenix appears—stating this charitably—a bizarre hodgepodge. Even the downtown no longer coheres: you remember scooting happily up and down the wide steps of those proud 1930s, art deco–ish buildings: now they look empty or bleakly dirty. Vagrants stagger past. The Westward Ho hotel, once a proud, clean crown of the young city, seems to be a flophouse. Charmless buildings careen in all directions, boxy, disjointed, abandoned, splintering. Some areas verge on slums.

But none of that seems to matter. Because the smells, the backdrop sightlines, the landmarks—Encanto Park, Phoenix College, Bob's Big Boy, Macayo's—the Arizona air (if Phoenix's is now mostly smog), beloved mountains, colors of the desert, place names—still stand, and for you they will be better than glamour. Will be like burying your head in your mother's pink-and-black checked apron, fragrant with toast and cigarettes and cold cream.

The landscape itself hasn't changed, but it has grown dowdier. Is it mimicking you, your generation, its unseemly symptoms of age? Phoenix has become a shabby chaos. Your husband says nothing, but you can tell he thinks it all a bit sad—and not a little boring.

Oh, please, nameless formless feckless gods of exhumation: help me get through this.

Now then, there is a way of being—in physical relationship to the earth—when you don't live near water.

That means you don't live near any natural body of water.

Desert, far as can be seen or imagined, is the given. The only known.

Dry, hard land. Pebbles, rock, sand. Limitless brush-dotted desert, seamed in the distance against purple-brown mountains at the edge of sky. Unchanged since the first lava cooled except to get beaten, whipped, cut, and compressed to grit or hardpack or Apache tears, the round black stone that—held to light—reveals itself to be translucent. (How you treasured your mineral collection, a cigar box whose inhabitants you'd carefully glued down, carefully labeled; quartz crystal, glittery-gold mica.)

When you grow up in the desert—when you grow up *upon* it— that thingness-to-thingness of body-to-earth, body ambulant upon inert dry sandy land, is coded into everything: the air, the ground, the body's awareness of itself, the carousel of conscious and unconscious in dreamy drifty swirl, fused at its taproot with the land—as if a skinny candle stuck into a cake *had started to partly become cake.* No rational reasoning about this osmosis occurs. It is wordlessly felt. The land stays itself. At the same time, it becomes part of you.

Until you go elsewhere, that's all you know.

I don't mean that the body thinks of itself as dry land, or that one's feet begin turning into sand. Rather, the body grasps the shape and weight of *itself* by *juxtaposition to what it touches*, what it moves upon.

The land is the medium, the informant. The medium *infuses* the body with self-definition.

I am body-upon-desert, body-upon-granulated rock, creosote, slate. Distinct but also porous—infused by the medium. One thinks and moves framed and filled by this settledness, this clean, calm aridity.

It's what we mean, in part, when we say we grew up in the West. That we're Western.

The earth beneath you (flowing outwardly from beneath your

feet) forms you and informs you, differently from any other place.

And yet you never once—not once—heard the word "landlocked" growing up in Sunnyslope, the northerly suburb butted up against low mountains. No alternative was visible.

One small such mountain, at the end of your childhood street, bears a big white S for Sunnyslope painted on it, an S as big as a football field. Local schoolchildren trek up there every year with buckets of white paint to refresh the giant letter. The S Mountain: oh, those words did make music. (Also the words *North Mountain Park, South Mountain Park*.) You and your sister scrambled around up there as kids, staring at the warm, known world spread below; the scrubby, khaki-colored, sand-and-pebble desert. Ants, lizards, an occasional horned toad, a beetle. Bones.

Dry, smooth, empty.

Once, though, a cave.

That's right.

You did not dream it. You and your little sister stopped one afternoon, in the midst of one of your aimless expeditions, when out of nowhere the thing gaped before us: a tall, black, open mouth in the high rock face we'd been skirting.

Gated. But the gate, a wreck of rust-encrusted metal, hung aside, drunkenly askew.

We sucked in our breath, staring. Then like puppies we tumbled, frightened yet incapable of resisting, as if by magnetic force, straight through that black mouth, coming to a halt just inside, trembling, gawking. Dirty red wax drippings festooned rock walls. The air was rank with staleness, old smoke, charcoal, dried straw, damp stone. You will never know *how* it happened, how you found your way there. But you will swear to any god that it happened— and oh yes, you'd heard about that cave. Local kids' gossip. And somehow, though no one is alive to witness and confirm, you found it. You stood together just inside it, shivering at the drastic drop in temperature though outside's afternoon rippled with heat.

Its Edgar Allen Poe name struck more horror into us than any monster on *Shock Theater*.

The Cave of the Iron Door.

For indeed—a heavy gate of dungeony metal fitted with pipelike rods, rust-crusted seams and studs, hung at a cockeyed angle, half falling off, from the cave's mouth.

Breath stopped, mouths agape, we edged deeper into the barely lit entrance. What walls we could see were smeared with candle-wax; air smelled of mildew, cold stone, dusty wax. My sister wouldn't go far past the cave's opening, though we dared each other on—into the black throat of the wide-open jaws, uninflected, unplumbable as the cave went deeper, becoming a real and true black hole: air colder and colder the deeper we went. That dank black chill, the quick absence of light the further in we crept, made us nearly crazy with fear, hearts tom-toming triple time. Soon we could bear it no longer and raced out screaming into welcome, desperately welcome, sunlight and air. Perhaps we'd just missed the adventure of a lifetime. Perhaps we'd just missed being dragged by demons to a grotesque doom.

Did we tell anyone? Did anyone believe us?

I cannot recall. It's no longer known. And now my adored baby sister, who might possibly have remembered, is also dead.

Oh, get those words down, friends. Get them down soon as you can. Talk to anyone who remembers. Get the words down.

We spent huge amounts of open-ended hours, Andrie and I, wandering those low, brush-covered hills, examining things without hurry or care. We had nothing but time, and no one worried about us. Surely you remember, too? From rising until supper, all the way to (dreaded) bedtime, was forever to a child. Summers were eternities. It wasn't unusual for kids to wander unsupervised all day, the neighborhood streets, the tranquil desert they abutted, desert where all streets eventually ended, where we studied bones and bugs, toads and lizards, inventing games, quests, projects; making up stories, singing, babbling. We tramped home to fix cheese sandwiches, and then set off again. It was a good childhood—by which I mean it felt good to us at the time, for a time, until childhood's abrupt end.

. . . in the time that I lived there so successfully disguised to myself as a child.

Who can convey it? You believed yourself, once, the legal tenant of a room called Childhood, living out what you supposed was a child's life—your sense of it—which meant infinite. You had little to remember: little from which to conjure. What others called a future seemed a curtaining mist. You were still dancing with your father by standing on his shoes as he shuffled side to side. The best fate you could dream of involved flying up into the lurid Arizona sunset–ravishing scarlet, pink, gold—with Paul Jones, a handsome boy in first grade who may or may not have been aware of your existence, to live in the clouds eternally as prince and princess: smiling and waving down at the adoring subjects of your earthly kingdom, nameless faceless kindly peasants who cheered the good-looking righteousness of the pair of you. As far as you knew, this pour of days, this cavorting over the pebbly hills, devouring hamburgers, paddling around the municipal pool, scrounging nickels for colas and candy, stepping side to side atop your father's shoes to Gershwin's *Embraceable You*—would go on and on.

Though you could never possibly, as a kid, summon such words.

You could sense (also without words) that your little mother seemed very sad. But you and your sister could not isolate or look too long at the word *sad*, let alone consider the why of it. Was her sadness our fault? For being too wild, too shrieky, for having tangles in our hair, for accidentally knocking down the planter lamp from the top of a bookshelf as we raced through the house, stopping to stare in horror, like unwitting murderers, at the clumps of spilled earth across the floor? For being too burger-and-ice-cream-craving, for not liking tomatoes or rice or lettuce or peas? For not falling asleep at once but calling out again and again in the dark for a glass of water just for the momentary reassurance of seeing at last her tired silhouette approach the bedside, reassure (shapely hands, silken skin, rose scent, low music of her patient voice) that no monster waited under the bed or in the shadows?

Was her sadness our fault, for not being good enough?

Our minds shut that door softly, and ran out into the scrubby desert to play.

I will say it again. The landlocked person is defined by the *ground under her*: a containment permeating all else. Earth is the fixative. The ground does not move. Earthquakes seldom happen in Arizona, or as The Arizona Republic phrases it, *Arizona isn't exactly a hub of seismic activity*. Houses there are often built to sit flat. Rarely does one see poles or scaffolding, and there's a vast, settled horizontalness in the ways structures are laid out, the ways areas for human use are organized—echoing the way the desert is organized, by geologic time. This layout defines lives. The dry, supine block-on-block-ness, the fact of no large body of water for hundreds of miles (canals, creeks, and swimming pools were cherished oases), flora that is tough, spiny or leathery but always brilliantly defended against drought and pitiless heat—those elements cast a person's body, a person's movement; her thinking, breathing, dreams.

Dreams are dry, mute.

Other people in other places grow up where water dwells, often noisily: constant, grand amounts of water. Walls of it. Falls of it. Places where water moves with force, cupidity, voluminous depth. Rooms of it. Tunnels of water, seething or flung or surging all year.

In the desert, by contrast, for movement we had dust storms: some so powerful and impenetrable that airplanes delay flights until they subside. One of them sucked all the roses off the vine fronting our tiny home, which made our mother, already fatally sad, sadder. Otherwise, in the desert, things stand still. Seasons are subtle but distinct; summers triple-digit but we kids spent them at the pool, turning dark brown, eating sugary greasy junk—or skipping back and forth through the sprinkler on the front lawn. Inside houses, evaporative coolers ran hose water, making an agreeable, damp, hose-watery smell and a faithful whirring that soothed. Winter air sharpened; colors sprang truer. Fall and spring hosted sudden displays of rainbow-hued cactus blossoms.

Elsewhere, lakes and rivers and oceans promise an escape route, even if you don't use them—their very presence gives reassurance, like that to a claustrophobe of sitting in an aisle seat. Water—even the distant scent of it—suggests an alternate medium nearby, for carrying you away. (Lives may of course also be lived upon and in and *beneath* big water.)

In the desert, most motion, therefore most escape, must come from the mind and body, invented and enacted by the body, against pure stillness.

The desert earth: a stillness like nothing else.

My poor mother, a New York native—that roiling city her only known world, her youth and childhood. Central Park, Coney Island, the magnificent Public Library; the beloved Met. Ten thousand shops and streets and characters, horse-drawn carts and jalopies, noises, smells; harbor, skyscraper, smoke and food and laundry; music in dozens of languages, vibrant crowds.

Imagine the erasure of all that.

Arizona in the 1950s must have seemed, to her, an alien planet—a terribly silent one.

She endured the dust storms—and once a flash flood, assaulting the desert after a sudden, hard rain. Because the parched land can't absorb it fast enough the brown runoff rushes down mountainsides into streets, creating a roaring river where a street had been. Kids on my street waded, amazed and thrilled, into racing mud-and-foam water that came up to our waists. After the flood, fat pink-and-gray earthworms materialized on our sidewalks like long pieces of flesh; pink question marks. Where had they come from? Where had they been (*what* had they been) before the rain? Why had they appeared now? What did they seek, or expect to accomplish? Why had they been born as earthworms and I as a human girl? I poked at the worms, watched their wet pink flesh flinch. Then I moved them carefully to the protection of lawn grass, hoping that would keep them from harm; they showed no inclination to protect themselves.

After the deluge, silence resumed.

My mother lived in that silence, imprisoned there.

She didn't turn on the television. She didn't play any of my father's (floor-to-ceiling shelves of) record albums, or the FM tuner on his sophisticated high-fidelity sound system, or even the big lunky Magnavox radio that he dragged into the backyard on Saturdays so he could listen to the Metropolitan Opera while grading papers (a T-shirt turbaned artlessly around his head against the sun). She rarely cleaned house, rarely saw or spoke to another living soul besides us little girls. When she wasn't driving us somewhere she sat at the dining table or on the toilet, eyes closed, a cigarette sending its single strand of white from between two fingers. We knew better than to bother her. She stood barely five feet, weighing less than a hundred pounds.

You and your husband park first at the hotel you've reserved in Scottsdale. Best to start at the border of things, work inward. Scottsdale, once a single, unpaved street lined with a handful of turquoise trinket and ranch gear outlets, is now a spreading grid of high-end clothiers, jewelers, malls, jostling providers of posh treats for the monied. Our hotel itself, one of those American names that have become a franchise, grouped toward the periphery of the town in a long parade of others like it, is a sprawling one with a couple of pools. You must drive perhaps ten minutes to reach Old Town, which turns out, once you arrive there, to appear harried and overrun: a surplus of stores featuring expensive, very bad art, much of it depicting scenes from a romantically imagined Old West. (One larger-than-life-size statue of John Wayne.) Streams of sports bars, cafes, diners of every ethnicity (Hawaiian, Cajun, Irish). Some claim to have been on the scene since the fifties—and en route, mile after mile of malls so identical they could be a recurring film backdrop. Palm trees. Saguaros. Traffic—far more than you remember or thought feasible. All we see are wealthy white retirees: often older women, thin and tan, taut, preserved, stalking the stores in pricey clothing, handbags, jewelry.

They seem to have nothing to do with the earth that bears them.

Scottsdale, in your childhood, was a dusty, one-street town with a few saloon-style shops (one sold saddles; another Levis Jeans, dark blue and board-stiff) and a single, matchbox-tiny art theater called the Kachina. There you saw *The Diary of Anne Frank*, your mother having hauled you and your little sister there—part of her perpetual search for purpose in the infinite, barren corridor of hours and days and months spent with two little girls and no visible husband.

You were traumatized by *Anne Frank* for the rest of your life.

Terrified. Stricken. The *eee-awww* of Nazi sirens (they sound the same in Europe today) will replay forever in your mind's ear—fanfare of bearing-down horror. You emerged into the hot Scottsdale afternoon blinded, bleached with fright. How you wish some wise muse had murmured into your poor mother's ear, *Marion, don't do this. Don't bring those little girls into this film: not yet. Give them twenty years.* Do anything else. Get them root beer floats.

But surely that same, impossible, wise muse would first have pleaded with my mother *Please live on, Marion: find a way.* Lift your feet up and forward through the tar. Find anyone to listen. Get help. Make a plan.

Who could have reached her? Who could have eased her?

Who could have made her listen? *Save yourself first, Marion. Secure your own oxygen mask before assisting the children.*

She was too shy, and too ashamed, to ask for help. In those days (still infiltrating our own) if a man strayed it was somehow tacitly considered a woman's fault—her inadequacy, her failure, or else the *what're-you-gonna-do* nature of men, for which there was no known remedy.

You just injected your grapefruit with vodka, her friend Berna told me later, *and shut up.*

Marion drove her two young daughters everywhere she could think of, places she knew nothing about. In those days you drove around and around and called it sightseeing. You looked at rich people's homes. Rich meant lawns: lush aprons of deep, cool, dark-emerald, manicured, beckoning grass. Deep, brilliant-green telegraphed money: money for gardeners, for extra water. Where was your father during all those drives, all that sightseeing, all those films, burgers, frostees, hotel pools, merry-go-rounds, acres of deep-green lawns?

Where wasn't he.

Latterly you have tortured yourself because it was him you worshipped. Your relief that it was not your father who'd died convinced you that you were a monstrous soul.

Did Bob ever phone Marion to tell her he was not coming home that night, or that he was coming home very late, or that he did not know whether he was coming home at all?

Berna reported he'd once shown up at her front door drunk, a hastily packed suitcase in his hand. She'd sent him home.

Did he make up stories? Would he suddenly appear at our house in such a drunken state he could not speak to explain?

You guess that all these scenarios were likely, by turns. You also guess you should feel thankful there was no car accident.

You heard them fighting sometimes. You'd be in bed; they'd assumed you were sleeping but you were lying awake in your darkened bedroom, your little sister sleeping across from you in her own small bed. It was a tiny house. Sounds from the living room boomed easily through the door into your room, reaching your ears like glass being smashed. You'd have given anything for it to stop. You feared that what you heard was somehow your fault. Her voice plaintive, wounded, beseeching. His, angry. What were they saying? Of what could he accuse her? Timidity? Shyness? True as charged. But (you now wonder, because the sounds made it seem so) why would he berate *her* for her gentleness in the face of his own cruel strayings, his own reckless, unappeasable hungers? He must have loathed himself, and her baffled grief must have made him loathe her more. All you could understand then was that the sound hurt your stomach. You could not make out the words. The sound was enough.

You worshipped your father. This made everything worse, impossibly complicated. He was handsome, tall, strong. He knew everything. He adored you—thought you gifted, beautiful, extraordinary. His belief made *you* believe those things. His voice was a cello's.

You fought with your mother toward the end. You talked back to her, aggravated and tormented her. Her own voice, once so musical, rasped raw at you as she stalked around the house in anger and exasperation. You were ashamed of her. You wished she dressed nicer and had her hair done more often. You wished she kept a nicer house. You wished there were more exciting things to eat in the kitchen, like the things other kids' mothers offered. You wished the bread in the breadbox wasn't a plastic sack containing a mushy loaf of generic white that looked as though someone had punched it. You had no real gear yet for looking deeper at any of this—yet conscious enough to feel sickened by your own evil nature, ashamed of your own shame.

Once, your dad entered the house after you'd been fighting with her. The silence was icy.

"Why is everybody so happy?" he asked mildly, after a moment.

The kindness in his voice sent you sobbing to your tiny bedroom.

You and your husband eat at an Italian place in Scottsdale, rigged with a gangster theme, with Sinatra and Dean Martin and similar types crooning all the standards on the sound system. Dark velvet covers the walls; framed photos of every famous Italian entertainer and mobster hang close together, like tiles. The place is raucous with tourists.

In fact, tourists overpower Scottsdale, especially during winter and spring. They move in packs on the street, piling into every restaurant and shop, every diner, bar, coffeehouse, and pub.

Tourists are often, you are bound to say, inordinately large-bodied beings. Their appetites seem limitless. They can pay for whatever they want.

Are we them? We're not that large, ourselves. But are we compounding their effect?

After a few nights at the Ramada, there's no putting off what must come.

The next stage is a lower-end hotel. You've no longer retained its name: on or near Hatcher Road, not far from your old Sunnyslope house. An odd area that looks—no other word for it—trashy. Luckily, your husband isn't finicky about hotels. This one is modern and clean. That's good enough. It's the *where* of the shelter that makes you feel slightly ill and unmoored, as if normal gravitational pull has gone aslant, which of course it has. You're visiting one future from a parallel future: the one before your eyes swims a bit, apparently blighted. We're staying in an area where, fifty years earlier, traffic noodled along at the base of those gentle mountains, not far from my grade school. Now the area is busy but also miracle-mile grimy and oppressed, a setting for a Ray Carver story. Day is hot, hazy. We find a barbecue place: *authentic*, we tell each other. It's strewn with sawdust. Waiters stream back and forth like ushers from a cashier's bullpen in the center, handing us a vibrating remote to alert us when a table will be ready. Inside is enormous, dark and loud, with screaming jukebox music that cannot, blended with the human clamor, be identified—we hold tight to our vibrating gizmo—and everywhere around us people are eating, shouting.

Certainly it *smells* authentic: intense barbecue smoke, drippings from pork fat, chicken fat, beef fat. I can't now remember the food. Both of us may be reflecting—silently—upon what our notion of authentic finally means. The barbecue place feels like a vortex of nowhereness, of down-and-dirty, of crapped-out pickup trucks and dog cages and well drinks, of bottom-line-scrapings, of often-divorced parents and neglected kids, of barely coping, boozed-out lives. We say nothing. I feel scared we may give off some telltale light or pheromone, marking us as liberal outliers—quavering lefties, or worse, intellectuals, eggheads—for which we'll soon, I fear, be singled out and punished. I am sure our expressions—at least mine—give us away. Vacantly hopeful. Hopefully vacant. Unitarians visiting the gun club.

How had my father and mother borne it, in the 1950s?

They hadn't. They couldn't. Each became differently lost.

My father became a drunk and a womanizer. (After you are older you'll look back and marvel that your father's yearning could have seemed mysterious to you. He wanted to feel alive, to transcend what was before him—though of course he himself had built what was before him. That's what people do, sometimes. Maybe more often than sometimes.)

There were multiple affairs. One resulted in a scandal at the college where he taught; confronted, he was forced to resign. That's when he secured the new job out of state, where my mother and my sister and I were planning to join him at the end of the school year.

We trudge back to our hotel, watch television. The next day I guide the rental car through hot morning light along the flat grid of streets, around the Little Hill (still there) to North Second Drive. Formerly Vista Bonita Road.

The street is a slum.

I can't do this. I have to do this.

First we drove—I drove us—to my grade school.

It was afternoon, toward lunchtime. Hot, clear.

I didn't need a map.

I could *feel* where I was, and where I had to go. I could *feel my way*. This flush of physical memory, power of an electric current—something altogether new—felt almost like a form of hysteria. Fierce internal radar commanded my arms and legs: this street, now this one. Turn here, now there. There's Tonya Thon's house. You passed it every single day walking to school. This corner is where the Texaco station stood—chevron-red as a cherry lollipop, stained auto-shop concrete, smelling forever of machine oil— where Pam Graves's dad, Tom, a tall skinny man with a crinkly smile and skin like beef jerky, worked on cars; made you feel special and singled out when, from behind whatever vehicle with its hood open, he pulled his head from engine surgery and waved, donning that crinkly smile as you both passed en route to school, making your way to the traffic light. Catty-corner across from that intersection was the drugstore where, if you were lucky enough to have a nickel, you sat on a stool at the soda fountain and ordered a chocolate Coke—indeed a paper cone cup of Coke with a shot of chocolate syrup in it. And if you were wealthy enough to find one more nickel you bought your favorite candy bar, a Snickers, to go with that healthful drink. These smells and tastes (the rich, wheaty-vanilla undersmell of malt) made a firmament, a close-fitting world—bracketed by the sound of the drugstore's screen door banging—then back out we went, under the hot Arizona sky.

You crept the car up the street and stopped opposite the enormous L-shaped recess yard where you spent your first seven years of playtime in grade school: at first somersaulting and dangling from the monkey bars, cleverly wearing shorts beneath your skirts, showing off; later strolling with friends, gossiping, teasing boys or pretending irritation when boys teased you, which actually meant love. All of it, you now understand, meant love—an anguish of love, hopeless and hopeful, a chaos of feeling seeping through your stomach walls while you entered the world each day, young raw registrars of the incomprehensible fact of the world, grappling to divine how to respond to the world.

You turned off the car engine. You and your husband watched the kids in the recess yard. They raced around in excited little herds, shouting; mostly Mexican American kids, just like their teacher, a kind-looking woman, plumpish, youngish, who coaxed and chatted with them as she bustled alongside them.

You murmur in wonder to your husband. "All the kids are Mexican now."

He nodded: "All the kids are Pakistani now, where I went to first form." He went to grade school in England.

You both sat with this a few minutes. Then you turned the car around, toward your old street.

Now I'm going to confess to you that there were two visits to this street, to this house.

The first happened many years earlier, with my beloved younger sister. We were in our thirties. Her two small sons came with us, bored and fidgety.

Bravely we drove. Bravely we stared at the house, parked across the street, through the glinting afternoon—a house now scarcely recognizable. The two palm trees that had stood like sentries at the front corners of the lawn were long vanished; even the butts of their trunks had somehow been razed or routed out. What had been lawn was now gravel. Heat paralyzed the air. Old plastic toys were scattered outside, scratched and cooking in the glare. Of the house itself we could scarcely make out the lines and borders once known so indelibly to us that imagining any other house anywhere always took the shape of this house.

We exited the car and marched to the door (the porch had vanished; likewise the trellis with its proud burden of rose vines).

The front door. Our front door. Same door? Surely not. Too fresh. We knocked.

A Caucasian man answered. He looked disheveled. T-shirt, shorts, hair askew. The cool breath from within that came at us was of cooking, the kind you smell in houses with children. Rice? Eggs? Oatmeal or macaroni?

He was a harried father.

My sister explained, breathless. We'd lived here once. Might we be able to have a quick look around inside our once home?

I stood numb beside her, unable to speak. My brain felt canceled in a barrage of static, obliterating white noise.

The man said yes, but without feeling. He opened the door and stepped back, gesturing us in.

We crept forward into the milk-smelling coolness, like the two little girls we'd once been.

Oh, remember them kindly in the time of their trouble, and in the hour of their taking away.

My sister never stopped talking. It was something she did, especially when she was nervous. She talked on and on at the man who let us in, while we stepped cautiously through the rooms—so small, those rooms—pouring out our history, which surely sounded like gibberish to him; it did in those moments to me, and love her as I did and do, I longed for her to stop talking. *Let us have this, please.* It was her way, wanting to include everybody, to take the world in her arms. While she jabbered I moved about like a sleepwalker, staring at the family's mess, seeing but not quite seeing, a queer sense of my own torso and limbs dissolving as I tried to fix memory over the solid surfaces before us—that corner the Hoffman television with its thick yellow screen; this wall the big Magnavox with the bright-chartreuse vertical line that moved sideways when you turned the tuning knob; here was where our couch had been, where they took the photo of toddling Andrie and little Joanie standing behind her; another corner had contained the small, folding, butterscotch Formica table where we ate—the way you'd align an old-fashioned photo negative's transparency over a color image. My sister's boys stood aside, patient, awkward, bored. My head felt crammed with sticky fog, like the pink cotton candy Andrie and I had devoured long ago at Encanto Park. And the droning in my head, a massive bee swarm's, grew louder and louder as I approached the bedroom that had been our parents.' Our mother had slept alone there so much of the time.

Labor Day, late morning, 1961. Our mother apparently still sleeping. Our father gone, beginning the new job in California. Cartoons on television. I was ironing, something I felt proud to do for the family. Andrie, age nine, couldn't find any cereal, and went to wake our mother to ask her where more might be kept. She came back, confused, into the living room where I stood ironing, saying our mother would not wake up. I rested the iron and went into the bedroom and she was lying on her side; her face seemed to sag very slightly toward the pillow; her lips, I will never forget, seemed a subtle but darkish blue.

I touched her arm. *Mom. Mommy. Momma, wake up.* The arm's flesh, coolish, gave softly, but the stilled form made no response.

Wrong. Wrong wrong wrong. That's all a kid's mind can hold or say. I can still feel what my heart did: as if it had been slugged or mashed, wheezing. I was eleven. I raced from the room out the door to the next-door neighbors: old Maurice Castle, who lived with his even-older mother. *Bang bang bang* on their screen door. Tall Mr. Castle appeared through the mesh of the screen, his Coke-bottle specs magnifying his alarm. *Please Mr. Castle can you come quick there's something wrong with my mother.* Without waiting for a reply I turned and ran back to my house. Maurice Castle and his mother came running straight out behind me (I heard their screen door bang); into my own house we strode. I led them to the bedroom. Mrs. Castle ventured in while Mr. Castle stood beside me outside the doorway to the room, his hand on my shoulder, gently staying me. And then at some signal from his mother—later I supposed her hands to have lifted in surrender like a bank teller's, her head perhaps shaking *no*, her eyes lit with horror—poor Maurice Castle's face went taut and pale and glassy and without any words he clasped me tightly to his scratchy-vested, camphor-ointment-smelling chest.

That was the room I came toward now, without will.

The door was closed.

Without asking permission I opened it, my sister's urgent voice cascading in the background.

Inside, alongside an empty bed, was a crib. In the crib, a baby slept.

I stared. I made no sound. The blankets around the sleeping infant were loudly colored and pilly, the light muted by curtains. The room smelled yeasty with sleep, of baby powder and old milk.

Soft silence, like the afternoon light.

I stared another moment.

I closed the door. I must have stood still a while.

We must eventually have looked at other rooms and made our expressions of thanks to the young father and exited the house and driven back to wherever we were staying.

I had to think a long time about what I had seen.

That it was possible for a baby to be sleeping where someone had died, where death had ended other possibilities—rerouted them.

New life could continue to gather itself, with normal ravenous fury, in the space where prior life had stopped.

The space made no objection—exuded no residual poison. Cast no hexing spell.

It was possible.

That had been the first visit.

The second was this one, with my husband, some thirty years later.

My sister is dead. Her sons are grown men rearing families of their own.

I pulled the car to the far side of the street, opposite the house. There it squatted, nondistinct, a miniscule ugly cementy tract home, a flat-faced pill in a vial of hundreds like it, the hundreds surrounding it in an oppressed, dusty, scrabble-ass neighborhood.

My husband waited, wordless, in the passenger seat beside me.

I didn't need to go into the house this time.

I could not bear it.

I buried my face against the steering wheel and sobbed.

It wasn't the desert's fault. I want to tell you that.

The desert was complicit by existing—but only that, existing. It had no agency.

Do places have agency? I think not. Places function as characters, as players; we assign them character and will: but they do not will. *We* are the will—or its lack.

A barbiturate was found in Marion's system, during the autopsy, matching a prescription issued for my father, who was tall and strong. It was never made clear whether the amount ingested was a deliberate overdose, or whether the dose taken had simply overwhelmed a tiny, weakened system.

It is possible your mother just wanted some sleep.

The surface couldn't have looked simpler. A brief getaway, some extra warmth at a chilly time of year. A visit to your old hometown—your *first* hometown.

People smiled, nodded.

Red State, Blue State

A Short, Biased Lament

The beginning's the thing.

That telltale beginning. I'm thinking now of a certain rocky pass we always find ourselves driving through, as we enter one of the red states. For some reason—as if by wicked plot—it's always a splendid, sunny day. The rock's natural formation acts like a tall corridor guarding the narrow pass. A delicious tension builds as we hum through this corridor—unable for a time to see anything but the strip of sky above us—aware that something temporarily beyond our sight is looming, about to break open.

We're changing atmospheres, crossing over.

The payoff, sure enough, is swift and dramatic. Once emerged from that steep-walled passageway we suddenly behold, out our front windshield, a vista resembling the Mormon vision of Heaven.

The moment wants a soundtrack, a surge of celestial music. At great distance, far below in all directions, spreads a blue-yellow-pink-green quilt of fields and farms and homes, peaceful and clean and fertile, like some painting of a promised land, depicting the best way humans might conduct their lives.

My throat closes; my eyes fill with tears. We stare spellbound at the tableau—a soft-focus illustration of peace and plenty. Chastened, both of us (husband and self) commence the kind of thinking each of us reliably reverts to whenever we're blindsided by beauty.

(Me: Time travel! Brigadoon! Why can't it be this lovely every-where?)

(Him: Wonder what it might cost to buy a small cabin out here, say just for summers?)

Be assured: when surroundings dazzle, Blue-leaning humans romanticize. We assume that a landscape's loveliness seeps into its inhabitants; that locals, infused by its power and glory, will show a caretaker's pride in the homeland—like park rangers or docents. A pristine setting must automatically mean a far-seeing, open-minded, openhearted people, right?

Oh, man. Why is the reverse so often true?

We drive on, still in awe. But the small visual cautions start to come into focus. Hand-painted signs, often shaky and misspelled, warn that property is private: trespassers will be made sorry. As we cruise slowly through main streets, it strikes us that no individuals of different colors or ethnicities seem visible except as service workers, confined to service-worker hidey-holes. Too soon some strange vibration begins to harass our minds like radio static, snaking through our bodies to exorcize awe and in its stead create what you'd have to call—putting this gently—a bad feeling.

Other trigger images swarm forward: a snarling bumper sticker. A neon Freeway Evangelism slogan, often in the form of a sour reprimand, lit up night and day on a roadside marquee. A series of political posters bearing hostile messages, planted in front yards or plastered against barns or propped against the chassis of defunct cars. A giant billboard drawing, jutting from the dusty furrows of agribusiness acreage, of Jesus's clenched, bleeding hand. It might be a monster truck roaring angrily past, flanked by two fluttering American flags as big as itself. This always gives me special grief—the flag stuff. So solemnly loved and pledged to, hand over heart, all my childhood—our beautiful flag has somehow been hijacked in recent years to come to symbolize a robotic, whitewashed, vicious patriotism, emblemized in turn by an extended middle finger and a single, familiar curse suggesting anyone who disagrees with the flag-flyer should vanish, or die.

I can feel our faces sagging. In the words of the GPS: recalculating.

The sinking feeling may sink faster with words uttered by a gas station attendant or a grocery clerk or a waitress—a glance or glare, a conversation overheard, a turn of language, a casually dropped slur—or the sight, in the midst of hardscrabble housing, of posh, gated communities encased by elaborate security, including an armed guard or two.

Both of us will feel the subtle poison commence its journey then, feeding like a slow-drip straight into the (otherwise gorgeous) air, land, water.

After that—and here's the deal—they're never quite the same, the land, air, water.

Even though they themselves have no opinions (only the instinct to exist), they're changed. You can never view them the same way because their beauty has become linked to a sensibility bent on hatred, exclusionism, and greed. Somehow the radiant earth and water have soaked up, and come to stand for, something dark and ugly.

This is when the car grows quiet. Road-trip bliss gives over to something else entirely.

We don't talk about it. After all, we've got our little Styrofoam cooler in the back. We've got the fruit and the sandwiches, the popcorn and the granola bars, cool road music, books on tape. We're theoretically high on adventuring, primed with expectations, lighting out for the territories.

Except we're now staring at landscapes and townscapes, feeling scooped-out.

Reader, we are made sad to visit the Red places.

Oddly, this flip-over happens afresh every single time. As if we've deliberately blurred out memory, so expectations can roll back to innocence between visits. But that innocence of ours is also driven, I think, by optimism. Margaret Atwood, author of a slew of graphically dystopian novels, noted in an interview: "Humans have hope built in."

For that reason, we venture into the Red zones hopefully—at first. Remember, they are often very beautiful. Mountains or lakes, desert or prairie: it begins breathtakingly.

Then it changes before our eyes, every time. No matter how majestic or serene or glittering it had first appeared, it reconfigures, grows brittle. Leering. Leached or, worse, rotten at the core.

We don't talk, after that second shoe falls. We keep driving, looking into the invisible middle distance, both of us working through our private clots of dismay.

I always start out wanting to suppose that we—Red and Blue— can surely, in an emergency anyway, reach each other: that we can do this easily and even cheerfully, across the obvious gaps. How we'd manage it, I reason at first, is by addressing basic human needs together: food, shelter, education. This naïveté gets slapped down fast; even hinting at those subjects can quickly launch an aggressive defense (junk food, trash culture, xenophobia, anti-intellectualism). It's only a short hop then from dismay to hopelessness, sometimes horror (shootings). The possibility that Red minds may ever arrive to any meeting with Blue minds—may ever want to—feels stillborn.

We joke sadly, en route, that none of this should be news. We nod together at the example of seventeenth-century satirist Jonathan Swift, who famously posited a war between two camps of otherwise civil-minded beings: they fought about opening boiled eggs at opposite ends. But Swift's send-up doesn't convey the modern stakes, the despair and fear we feel. Those endless egg wars did not, in Swift's telling, threaten the whole damned planet, a threat growing larger since (at this writing) the 2016 American presidential election.

Home is suddenly looking better and better.

Berkeley-based author Arlie Hochschild, in her Pulitzer-nominated investigation *Strangers in Their Own Land*, interviews the grown sons and daughters of a deeply Red region, many of whom have lived all their lives in environments ruined by corporations they still support—people who often demand (and receive) regular help from a government they openly, sometimes violently despise. And while I sympathize with Hochschild's discovery—that these men and women feel betrayed by everything including their own ideals, relying upon religious notions for assurance of pending (if postlife) relief—I cannot catch a glimmer of the hope that Hochschild seems to hold, for connecting in some fruitful way with them.

We're talking about Hochschild's shiny ideas as we cruise past drugstores, big-box stores, fast-food franchises. American flags line the streets. Meth addicts and fundamentalists line the back roads.

Of course we all know Blue friends who, for reasons of work or family, must live in Red states. They cope with the strain and loneliness in different ways—creating a cocoon of the home base; networking with like-minded types; flinging themselves at projects, exercise, charities. They schedule intervals of escape. Not least, they pick their battles. (If there's no protest march where you live you organize one or travel to one. If the campus where you teach decides open-carrying of weapons is fine, you make sure students know your office doubles as a safe space, that you'll help anyone feeling targeted, and so on. You lobby and demonstrate for better legislation. You quietly hunt for a job in a Blue community. You drink.)

Sometimes you just throw up your hands and leave. I have those friends, too.

We also know that fortresses of Red sometimes dwell, against odds, inside Blue, and vice versa; that a few states are so fiercely divided as to create a bizarre, two-headed effect. We think of them as bipolar. Within one state, pockets or strips of okayness may exist, tiny arty villages where we step from the car for a bite or a stretch and the cautious initial vibe is this-feels-do-able. Pockets or strips also exist where, when we stop to ask directions at the nearest bar, the message telegraphed soundlessly is *get the hell away fast as you can*. We jump back into the car and gun it out of there.

How did this distribution come to be?

My husband points to what he calls early "settlement patterns." Rural or sequestered areas, left to themselves, tend to seal off, suspecting the Other (any Other) as a possible marauder. Whereas townships and cities (living in closer proximity, expecting influx and egress, sharing services and systems) are more often forced to cooperate, giving leeway by logical deferral, assuming resources will be pooled and divided to benefit the larger whole. These are generalizations, but a clear peal of truth rings from them.

What can't be ignored is that certain places sooner or later make us feel unwell. In turn (despite our best efforts), that can forever skew perception—shrinking and soiling, somehow, that place's very place-ness.

In some crazy way, that's the part that hurts the most.

It's not the place's fault.

So when our tour is done and we find ourselves at last driving home back through the rocky pass?

By that point we don't notice weather, or care. We can't wait to see that pastel-quilt, bible-story panorama recede behind us till it disappears. When it does, the wash of relief contains a pang of shame—but also a sense of loss.

What was lost? An idea. An ideal. The beauty didn't translate. It didn't carry over.

Some will scorn these thoughts as mere wrinkles in the silken duvet of white privilege. True: there's no escaping the bitter reality expressed by people like Ta-Nehisi Coates (born in crack-maddened Baltimore) of an America that so hates and threatens black bodies and lives, the owners of those bodies and lives feel they have no choice, whenever possible, but to gather their kids and flee.

Yet other countries suffer similar realities. At this writing the United Kingdom wrestles with Brexit. Germany faces the rearing cobra of a resurgent, immigrant-scapegoating right. So do Holland and, of course, France. And those are first-world models!

It makes you want to hang a "Temporarily Closed for Renovation" sign on the planet. "Thank you for your patience! Watch this space for our new, improved design!"

But people don't seem able to stop being born, growing up, and having babies themselves. All of them want to make good lives. Maybe that's where our best shot has to lie.

"Humans have hope built in."

Today I Will Fly

We take airplanes everywhere now, casually as crossing the street.

Airplanes are also understood to be the worst polluters of Earth's atmosphere.

We still do it. Everyone, just about, who can afford it. I don't really understand this but I do it right along with them, several times a year, short hops and long. People high-five you for it, admire it—assume it. As if by silent, instinctive agreement, no one seems to think twice. If I *were* to think twice, I'd guess that bringing up the cheery topic of eco-betrayal won't make many friends. No one among those in my circle quips, *Reckon I'd better take an ocean liner or train so as not to mess up the biosphere.* (Liners and trains probably don't help the planet's health, either. They also tend, strangely, to cost a lot.)

Never mind. The fact of flight is touted, in all media, as a reward, luxury, adventure; as hip and chic and, never least, the vital sign of a flexing spirit. ("My parents are still cool; they fly everywhere!")

No airline tacks onto its advertising, for an afterthought: *oh yes, we're also producing a carbon trail that's adding hopelessly and irreversibly to the climate change that's freaking out the world right now and probably damning future generations to an atmosphere like that of Mumbai, where you can't see across the street and people are besieged by incurable lung diseases, but whatever.*

Instead, a symphony of bragging strikes up every day on social media, with billions of photos and videos documenting real-time, real-place junkets. *Here I am in*—take your pick. Quito. Firenze. Prague. Paris. Iceland. Granada. Dublin. Singapore. London. Santiago.

I am blessed, the captions read. *I love my life.*

There's generally but one way those people got there.

Sometimes they photograph their legs and feet and bags in airport bars and lounges. They post photos of their meals and drinks there, too. Does it make me pine to do what they are doing?

Nope.

In principle I am thankful for air travel, though I still pray at every takeoff and landing. (Despite ten thousand successes, this might be it, the sudden announcement of my number in the heavenly roll call.) Flying is so peculiar, so singular: the one event in which a person temporarily but indisputably floats beyond earthbound obligation, beyond the gravitational laws of an organized social system—for that matter, beyond reach of its opposite, war and anarchy. All ties, all debts (emotional, financial) cease for that interval in the air. No one can *get at* you, for a little while.

I think of the young protagonist in Simon Van Booy's astonishing novel *Everything Beautiful Began After*: insane with grief following the death of his beloved in an earthquake, he withdraws all his money from the bank and begins taking any airplane anywhere, hopping onto any next flight in any direction as soon as he's landed. He just flies and flies, around the clock and through the days.

I can see that. I can understand it.

I know I am not the first to wonder whether, as a byproduct of flying, the mind may enjoy special powers—among these perhaps the power to think differently, better, clearer, more deeply. And certainly I wonder, as a writer, whether insights that wouldn't otherwise exist might be extraterrestrially conceived: as if in some soulful café, except airborne. So we scribble away, full of breathless awe for the fact that the Cloud Muse is guiding our hand. Too often, back on land, we haul out our magical scribblings to stare at them—and they're the babblings of a schoolgirl's diary.

Maybe I've got it backward, and we're blinkered up there.

Conditions are altered, yes: an eerie feeling of passing through a time-space slot that's not, strictly speaking, our own. At least one *Twilight Zone* episode considered this. (A flight had "mistakenly" landed when it should have been lost, and its passengers thereafter one by one disappeared. The horrifying implication: some other dimension was claiming them.) I think also of *Lost Horizon*: its shivery hint that plane travel may take us to, or through, parallel but otherwise inaccessible dimensions.

Oddly, observation suggests the reverse; that thinking in the air veers instinctively toward basic, physical comforts. A kind of animal awareness takes over: where to put your legs; what kinds of people surround you and how best to endure them; how best to navigate food, drink, sleep, access to the toilet.

As for chic? My husband points to the hordes of exhausted, smelly passengers and their screaming kids, elbowing each other as they file in and out, rearranging themselves, grappling to yank cases and duffels and packs from overhead bins, trying not to bonk each other on the head; waiting in cramped, damp, rumpled huddles for the cabin doors to open like refugees who've crouched in steerage, waiting to be liberated.

It's not an image the airlines reproduce. Only the news channels do that, when strikes and weather cancel flights.

My husband notes drily, "Whoever invents a solution to this will make millions."

Yet after all these years—all the bewildering pain of modern travel—there's still something thrilling about boarding a plane.

The head-smack occurs when you glimpse that little crack of light between the mouth of the walkway tunnel and the aircraft's open cabin door. Down through the spilling light you can clearly see, far below, the concrete tarmac.

You think, oh man.

You're doing something drastic. You're about to change environments in a shocking, science fiction way. And the interim inside that big, thrumming tube with its tiny rows of lights and choreographed speeches and sample oxygen masks and exit doors and folding plastic trays and disinfectant smell—the sacred, locked-off cockpit, from which a captain's voice purrs on the sound system as if he or she were giving a fireside chat—thrusts you into a science fiction world. Disorienting, arbitrary—why *can't* I hang out near the galley kitchen?—the phenomenon might as easily be some sustained, collective dream: zooming through the sky at gazillion miles per hour at a "cruising altitude" (such easygoing words) of gazillion feet, across time zones it once took months and years to traverse, in a silver bus weighing tons but going so fast that it rises and (pray to every god) stays risen.

We will not speak of those instances where it does not (stay risen). We just won't.

My husband, who above all things adores travel, is terrified of flying. I don't find this illogical. He takes a generic prescription, the equivalent of Valium, before boarding. (I decline the medication because one of us will need to think crisply and possibly drive us somewhere, on arrival.) It works well; he's often dozing by takeoff. I can only feel thankful the sedative was invented. Now we mainly contend with the exhaustion and jetlag of long crossings. (They're often long; he has family overseas.)

But we do it. We fly and fly. He needs travel like food. It's nonnegotiable. Whereas I dread it. I want to live in my pajamas. So I pick my battles: I'll go to this place with him, not that one. (He'll go with a friend to that one.)

And on we fly. I'm accustomed, as family secretary, to booking the trips: analyzing websites, seeking cheap fares, nonstops, redeemable miles. It's I who make the satellite-aided calls to reps in India and Ireland; I who wade through frustrating, echoey exchanges that are difficult to hear or understand and cost us extra for the privilege. I'm accustomed to marshaling all my spiritual and physical mojo to withstand what I know, in a very *best*-case scenario, lies in store: the long stretches of waiting in lines; the wands and pat-downs and random baggage searches by security personnel; the droll, bored eyeflick assessment by customs officials; the conveyor belts and walkways and incomprehensible public address announcements; endless lugging; furious concentration hunting down and deciphering signage; smells of coffee and fried meats and sugar, perfumes and booze, cigarette smoke and stale bodies—including our own. The sour taste in our mouths.

Followed by more tramping, more lugging, bus rides, train rides, maybe a ferry now and again—but always, always, another plane.

The real-time tracking map on the seatback video screens shows a tiny symbol-plane, representing yours, edging with numbing slowness (even at gazillion miles an hour) across the North American continent. Mapmakers color the screen's landmasses a dark, rich green, with striations implying texture. If you're heading further, the symbol-plane then moves over Greenland, into Europe, across China, Russia, and so on. The oceans around these landmasses are colored a stunning, deep blue, which somehow conveys the sea's majesty and depth, even in miniature form, mysterious as outer space. In fact you're also seeing outer space itself beyond those seas: the heavens are black. This seems fitting, if not consoling; perpetual, infinite, unknowable night surrounds the blue planet you're crawling over.

And the biggest reveal? It's not on the screen. It's out the window. Look down.

See the mountains and lakes, the lights, the bridges, the earnest cities, patchworks of farms and fields, spreading suburbs (their tiny, bright blots of turquoise pools).

There's our story, illustrated.

Our predicament. Our best stab at a (semi-)functioning civilization.

See the great stretches of salt, the Rockies, the snaking Mississippi, the proud clustered skyline of Manhattan. That's our turf, where we were born and thrash through our days, and where we will die. Previous generations never got to see this, to digest it through their eyes. See the weather you've lifted above or now descend through; the Raphaelite piles of silver cloud; the sudden, blackening storm. Glimpsed from above, that panorama of where we have lived and roamed from the very beginning—the layered air that quilts or buffets us while we struggle through our lives, wondering what any of it may mean, and what to make of ourselves—hits hard.

Something's *almost* understood then. We come *just* to the edge of an understanding, and waver there. It's like hearing a passage of sublime music, or listening to the wind stir the trees, and feeling yourself closing in on—what? The essence of something—ineffable, even godly.

You reach with all your mind and heart, gazing down, straining to grasp it.

But then the pretty puzzle—buildings, highways, runway lights—starts rushing toward us, closer, bigger, less contained, duller.

Then *whoosh* and *thump*, and we're back. The engines do their alarming slam of reverse-thrust—whammo—and that quivering, incandescent filament of quasi-meaning, vanishes. Instantly we've lost or forgotten the near godliness, the almost-got-it, whisked-away answer to a question we never quite knew how to ask.

We're thinking instead about checking the cell phone and yanking the overhead bag before others yank theirs, and don't forget your hat-sweater-coat and will there be time to pee and still make the connection and can we please get the hell out of here now, please, off this plane.

Was that briefest near epiphany worth any of the rest of it?

It's probably not a fair question, because that's not, strictly, why we set out. Our purposes tend to be more . . . prosaic.

I do, though, keep thinking about Simon Van Booy's grief-stricken young man who flew and flew, so as not to have to touch the (pain-giving) planet. That image haunts for a reason: it is telling us something.

For a rejoinder, I think of the end of a Robert Frost poem called "Birches"; though the whole thing is beautiful, the end is what I like best:

I'd like to get away from earth awhile
And then come back to it and begin over.
May no fate willfully misunderstand me
And half grant what I wish and snatch me away
Not to return. Earth's the right place for love:
I don't know where it's likely to go better.

Little Traffic Light Men

You can't wish away a lifetime's conditioning—movies, print, Saturday morning cartoons—as if it were some dismal weather system. At least this time, after twenty-two years away from Germany, the language sounded more comic than not. Something-*fährt* was printed on a huge airfield building as we taxied in on a sunny May morning, and something-else-fährt on another. That cheered me.

So this time (clenched into a wad of aching muscles on the nonstop from San Francisco, tramping the sprawling, halogen-lit maze of Frankfurt Airport) I meant to push aside reflexive dread. Time is ripe, I thought, to flip that trope. I already sensed that confronting the language, and everything it once evoked, might no longer knife me.

Surely it would feel easier this round. Enough years had passed. A new generation had grown up—now itself busy making babies. Things would have changed. Germany, I reasoned, would step forward to meet me more than halfway.

I also longed to be taken out of my own head, made to look outward. Read on.

The last time my husband and I walked on German soil was in 1994. The wall had tumbled only five years before. Five years, in the staggering-to-its-feet of a war-raked city, is not a lot. Sun filtered through pale and weak on our first day there: early spring, exceedingly cold, and Berlin looked and felt like a plane crash. Air held a dazed, floating-motes aftermath. People's faces appeared locked as they hurried past, scrubbed of any readable inflection as they swayed from handheld straps with the tram's roll. Cold spaces. Hard surfaces. Conventional niceties nowhere visible. Bullet holes peppered many walls. Alexanderplatz yawped wide and barren then, an abandoned military concourse, windswept and freezing, the infamous radio tower stabbing from it like a spear, its concrete emptiness a space we could too easily fill, in imagination, with platoons of goose-stepping, helmeted troops—or worse.

We wandered that day, confused; no sense of a *there* there. Only hodgepodge. Bricks and rubble. Canvas half draped a gaggle of life-sized statuary huddled at the rear of a vacant lot behind chain link fencing, like a crowd of refugees trying to shelter itself. West Berlin, on its surface, felt no more appealing or friendly, no easier to navigate or make sense of, than East. It was only more expensive.

Some disclosure is in order. Because of my last name and vague sense of family background (my late folks had no more truck with Jewish orthodoxy than an occasional sip of sweet kosher wine), and because of the fifties and sixties I grew up in—that era's haste to push off from the past, get on with things—I'd guarded all my life a secret terror that fascism, in the form of a resurrected Nazi machine, could spring back at any time, fast and stealthy as a cancer. Never mind I had no clear idea why an evil cabal wanted to kill people bearing my last name. It had done so once; it could again, wasting no time taking over my country and the world. A child could only build upon what she'd grasped in the first ten years of life, from a range of half buried allusions and images. Thus, all people of Jewish background (however dimly I understood that) would, in my secret nightmare, be hunted down, rounded up, and destroyed in ways I had read about or seen enacted in films—starting with *The Diary of Anne Frank.*

I remember, in those growing-up years, feeling dizzy with it, the blank noncomprehension: How could the kind, loving grown-ups of this world allow what I'd read about, and what I'd seen that film suggest, subtly but terrifyingly, to happen? How could it have been real—even conceivable?

My little sister and I attended Unitarian Sunday school. We trick-or-treated for UNICEF on Halloween.

Yet before that selfsame world, findable in any library, was *The Diary of a Young Girl*—breathing quietly beneath its shroud of reverence and fear and, yes, titillation. All references to the diary, to the history inseparable from it, made the book itself seem transgressive, hot with controversy, unspeakable implications. Even as a kid you couldn't not be shot through with queasiness for the reverence, as much as for the implied unspeakable. Somewhere I'd seen photographs, been unable to look away. Living skeletons, hollowed-out animals dying behind cage bars. Tall piles of bony corpses, great mounds of bodies shoveled onto one another by steam shovel. Arms and legs and feet and ravaged faces sticking out of these piles, mouths frozen open. Tattooed numbers. Piles of gold teeth, wedding rings. Six-pointed yellow stars. Crushed humans by the millions. Families. Children.

This really happened?

All of it juxtaposed by turns against black-and-white snapshots of the young diarist's face: sweet, sunny, framed by dark curls above her Peter Pan collar.

My ten-year-old eyes stared at that photo again and again. She'd have loved, I guessed, all the stuff my sister and I loved. She'd have had favorite songs, favorite books, games, a bracelet or necklace, a sweater; maybe a cigar box for keepsakes, an acorn, a marble, a piece of ribbon. I remember trying as a child to imagine how she'd have looked after she and her sister were devoured by the camps: heads shaved, lice-ridden, starved and freezing, death by typhus.

That part, of course, doesn't appear in the film. All you see at the film's end are the characters looking quickly at each other after the fatal alert has reached them. Their hopeful, pitiful gambit, hiding silently in an office attic for two years, is up. Their glances at one another in final moments, like the squeeze of a hand, telegraph their nod to the incomprehensible: *This is it.* Someone in Amsterdam has tipped off the authorities; the SS knows the group's whereabouts and is at that moment bearing down upon them. Awareness is sharpened by the approaching sound, louder, louder, of the two-note German police siren—*eee-aww eee-aww*—a hellish, hysterical braying.

My child's mind would always shut down at this point. (How my poor little sister's mind ingested what we'd seen, I can't imagine. We wouldn't have known how to speak of it.)

My adult mind wants to shut down, too—but it's packed with images, the kind that pop up to terrorize at 3:00 a.m. for the rest of your life, scored by the soundtrack of that siren.

To this day the crazed screaming of European police-car sirens—that two-note wail, that high-pitched, frantic *eee-aww*, unchanged it seems since the war—still has the power to stop the heart, shatter thought, atomize reason like a lightning bolt. It's an aural marker and fanfare of death's jaws gaping, a sound I can never completely dissociate from *they are coming for me*. Can never flush the closed throat, the adrenaline prickle, the bunched fists and stuttering heartbeat. Can never pretend I am coexisting calmly, indifferently, maturely, with that sound.

We flew into Frankfurt first to visit my stepson, a wonderful young man stationed nearby as part of his military duty. It seemed the right moment for revising the dread that surely now no longer fit. I had rolled up mental sleeves, determined to sweep out biases, see things new. We had all lived—Germany and the world—into new news. Twenty-seven years had passed since the end of the wall. Other horrors now darkened our planet's once-clean heavens: climate change, ISIS and Al Qaeda, belligerent viruses, internecine tribal atrocities, refugee crises, insane assassins armed to the teeth, maniacs and despots seizing power. Meantime, in Germany, a full generation had come of age—one that appeared well educated, matter-of-fact about even the worst aspects of the realities they face, willing to invent something better.

Now comes the "what I supposed versus what I learned" recital. The German contingent of this (my stepson's) millennial generation, from what I thought I could discern without language, seems to respect the old nightmare—granting that the nightmare's after-images still grip aging survivors in bloody talons. But the young adults also seem determined to consider it ancient history, the kind discussed in textbooks. They publicly consecrate the memory of the murdered (now the official word), pledging and re-pledging themselves, in monuments and speeches, to exemplify vigilance, to safeguard human rights. Markers and museums of every aesthetic, insisting we never forget, crop up everywhere. In Mannheim our son led us to a glass booth on a busy thoroughfare, whose walls bore a kind of foggy translucence. At closer glance this fog turned out to be inscription, in tiniest letters, of thousands of lightly printed names covering every inch of the glass. A brief scan confirmed that most of those names were, like mine, recognizably Jewish.

We stood there a moment, running our eyes over column after column.

Each name someone's beloved darling, now a cloudy mark on glass in a bustling city.

We walked the tidy districts and neighborhoods, seeing the young (like their counterparts elsewhere) absorbed by the daily, the necessary pleasures and tasks: showing up to jobs; rearing kids; building communities; savoring arts, sports, landscapes, food, friendship. These people looked smart, humane, preoccupied with survival, hoping (like any species in progress) to make things better.

They were parents, harassed and proud and tired, pushing strollers or calling toddlers to their sides in parks, cafes, fast-food outlets, sidewalks. They were self-styled bohos, smoking and chattering amid the litter of beers and coffees. They were musicians, painters, boutique owners, bookstore and retail clothing clerks, grocery checkers, museum guides, landscape and building maintenance and construction workers, teachers, researchers, drivers, waiters and waitresses, nurses, cops and firefighters, nannies and caregivers, highway repair workers. ("There are two seasons," our son told us: "Winter and Road Work.") They were students, rumpled and sleepy, flirting in parks, playing horns or guitars or cellos, sketching in museums; they were old guys perched patiently on stoops or in cafe chairs or on benches. They were tourists exploring palace grounds, forests, scenic lookouts, truck-stop restaurants, patiently escorting aging parents, explaining, cajoling. They coached and scolded and laughed at their own kids.

I felt no darkness from them. No perfidy. No scorn. Of course I stood outside the culture, outside the language, but say what you will: humans emit force fields that can often be felt and heard and, to some degree, read. I looked and listened. Young bohos in the Germany I glimpsed appeared identical with young bohos in comparable settings; kids and babies and parents as you'd expect to find them. I cannot claim to have felt great warmth from these individuals, but courtesy and mildness ruled. Sometimes strangers offered to explain a sign or menu, or clarify directions. Our son drove us through Mannheim, Karlsruhe, Nuremberg. I swallowed hard at the sound of that latter name, but the Nuremberg we saw presented as cheerful and handsome, oblivious to the day-of-reckoning thunder its name once evoked. The city has proudly rebuilt itself almost completely—even its cathedrals, which manage to look centuries old.

We found wellsprings of charm and beauty in Bamberg, its genial mix of locals and visitors, cafe culture, vine- and flower-covered, saggy gingerbread homes along the river, fairy-tale style. An aged man with thick white hair and patrician features leaned out a high window to prune his roses; the blooms were fat, round and velvety, peach-red. Squinting up as we walked past, on impulse I called out to him that his flowers were beautiful. (This was something my sister would have done, along with stopping to pet and croon at every dog and baby.) The aging man nodded wearily as if enduring a stale gesture, as if he heard those words every day. At once my impulse felt smartly checked. Who might he have been, in a prior century? Who might I have been, as part of the population surrounding him? Might he have as wearily targeted me, or the family or compound that harbored

me? Might I have been but one of a steady stream of undesir-
ables, as steadily and casually singled out for exile—or extin-
guishment?

During the hours I strolled past the gingerbread homes and
hand-built fences along the river, all of it covered with thick-twining
roses—afterward sitting down to *trocken* (dry), crisp white wine in
an outdoor cafe packed with families, couples, students, shouting,
exuberant—those questions pulsed below the more mundane concerns: where we might next walk, what we were presently seeing,
which photos to snap. I pushed the dark questions down before
they could unfurl in pretty daylight.

What, I wondered then and wonder now, has second-guessing
ever truly served?

It can be argued two ways.

One: Assign no meaning more sinister until there's evidence
for it.

The other?

Assume the worst. *No point second-guessing* is what lots of
people told each other in the years and months leading up to
1939, to Kristallnacht. Thoughtful people—good, smart people—
counseled family and friends. *Calm down. Be reasonable. Wait
and see. No need to panic; just wait a while. It will come right. It
will sort itself out.*

Despite those prickling reverberations—inflamed now by the
election, in the year of this writing, of perhaps the most frightening
protofascist ever to assume office in American history, with terrifying implications for the nation and the planet—despite those, I
confess that in the halcyon days of touring with our son (and later
by ourselves in Berlin) we took refuge in a mental condition we've
nicknamed *a spazz-out of happiness*: meaning the arbitrary erup-
tion of a heightened state; antic, glazed, willed jubilation. *People
are good at heart. History rights itself.* Life and objects may be trundling along having logical, discrete identities and trajectories
unconnected with other matters. But the perceiver's spazz-out cor-
rals, connects, and infuses all it spies in that moment with the

meaning necessary to serve the need. The Happy Story we tell ourselves can be a bully and a brute—something Americans do especially well. We do it best, in fact, while we are tourists. We've invested a lot in our story. Self-image. Money. Fear.

Fear of what, you ask?

Why, fear of the jolly story being otherwise.

Were it otherwise—*they might be coming for me.*

Was any of this grim internal tabulating fair to modern Germany? Did Germany know or care? Of course not. What is Germany or any nation-state but an aggregate of individuals, each toting her and his aggregate of needs, touched inadvertently by pieces of common history and current culture? Germany as a collective consciousness cares most at any given moment—like any other generalized group—about survival; as a close second, about a quality of survival. Each person in its fold, infant to elder, wants to feel well, do well, thrive and prosper.

All the rest? My imposition. My ascribing.

But isn't this the way any traveler moves through the world?

As noted earlier, weather still calls the shots. Never doubt this. Whatever weather happens to be doing wherever we happen to be traveling, that place *becomes* that weather, in memory. If we're stuck in Blackburn, England, in January and the dirty snow outside and bitter-freezing temperatures make my husband's father take one look out the window and climb back upstairs to tunnel back into his bed, that will forever be Blackburn in my brain's illustrated dictionary. If I am a twenty-year-old living in a Peace Corps trainee dorm in Dakar, Senegal, when sudden rains hammer the corrugated roofs like poured nails—and when five minutes later the soaked earth roils steam into a sky white again with boiling sun, while the smell of pummeled leaves and dirt and feces and rotting mangoes and baked bricks and grease and gristly meat smoke fills my skull—that's the permanent imprint, no matter how many years ago it happened. In my mind's album of emblematic scenes, that will be the diorama floating forward, replete with grit and humid stink.

But recent scenes can, and do, eclipse their predecessors.

So when in Berlin, twenty-two years after our freezing first visit, with its plane crash tableau, we step into a Georgia O'Keeffe painting—a bright-blue sky filled with marching bands of cotton-puff clouds—suddenly *that* becomes the new template, the forever-picture of Berlin (maybe of all of Germany) in the brain's archive.

Come with me into the present tense now. My husband and I have traveled here after visiting our son, to have a swath of time together in this city we scarcely remember.

Our venture seems blessed by weather. As if weather were the Pope in an extremely good mood, it has palmed the crowns of both our heads and declared, *Guys, this is gonna be a bell-ringer. I guarantee it.*

We know it the moment we step out of the train into the towering interior of the Berlin Hauptbahnhof, a megalopolis of a station serving (from the looks of it) the whole universe. Google it: the Hauptbahnhof is a symbol, a machine, kinetic art, a multilevel hive; its entire front wall—three sky-piercing facades—a flashing quilt of blue glass. Not least, the station serves as a multiplex shopping mall, whatever you may think of that—several levels of store upon store offering home decor, clothing, jewelry, pharmacy sundries, sports equipment, chocolate, crystal, groceries, booze. *This is how we do it*, the German sensibility seems to be declaring. Monolith of glass and steel: seen through half-shut eyes, the structure resembles some hokey science fiction conjuring. Hordes push through in all directions around the clock; people wend their bicycles through swarms of walkers. Frenzied, roaring futuropolis—and once we manage to thread through the exit doors and step outside, the beauty of heavenly weather falls over us like silk.

Shining City! Hope of men!

Because we have allowed ourselves certain occasional luxuries at this stage of our traveling lives, we take a cab to the hotel. Through its windows we gawk at clustered skyscrapers, thronged

streets, motorbikes, babies, cafes, businesses, tourists—and everywhere against that sky for 360 degrees, gargantuan building
cranes, moving with slow determination like some giant, benevo-
lent aliens tending the expansion of their earthbound nest. Everything is bathed in steady sun. It is June. It is warm. People zoom
around on bicycles.

Spazz-out goes into overdrive.

We loved everything we saw. I can itemize highlights or you can
read about them from Rick Steves. Art: dazzling, brilliantly show-
cased. Architecture: handsome, stately. Streets and parks and
buildings: historic and modern, almost always immaculate. Energy:
crisp, strong, exhilarating. Ambience: a festive air of good will
toward men, fortified by abundant, delicious beer and wine. (Excellent coffee, bakeries, fish.) Best of all, the rollicking momentum of
this feckless bien-être felt punctuated and buttressed at every turn
by the regular, larger-than-life appearances, inside the cylindrical
cones of traffic lights—of a remarkable figure.

Actually, there are two of them: quite different.

The stocky, bright-red little man faces you, both arms stretched
wide to indicate, unmistakably, *no no, go no further!* Whereas the
walking little green man is silhouetted, midstep, from the side, so
you can appreciate his long, confident stride. Both men appear to
wear a pork-pie hat. Except on the red guy, who faces us, it looks
more like a helmet. But if it *were* a helmet, it would not (I must
insist) be a soldier's. It would be the helmet of civic duty: that of a
crosswalk guard or civil defense volunteer.

Reader, I must now politely request you grab your smartphone
to view, on the Internet, these images I so powerfully love. (Permission issues forbid reproducing them here.) Then allow me (assisted
by Wikipedia) to introduce Ampelmänchen, Little Traffic Light
Men, created in 1961 in then-East Germany "by traffic psychologist
Karl Peglau (1927–2009), as part of a proposal for a new traffic
lights layout . . . "

Ampelmann! My new best friend. Symbol—especially in his
green version—of a friendly friend who cares for my safety—and

much more. Ampelmann signals not just *when* it is time to go forward but—pay attention please—*how*. Do as he does, he seems to be urging. Set forth with resolve, with fullhearted expectation.

All that's often given to us to control, we're often reminded, is our own response. Response to the unspeakable, the ineffable, the unknown. Ampelmann *enacts* a best-of-all-possible response, one that recalls the late E. B. White's analogy for commencing to write an essay: namely, going out for a walk. (One envisions White's cheerful *ur*-essayist venturing forth in exactly the posture of green Ampelmann, alert, friendly, spirited.) Call this state of mind, say, forwardism, a preemptive *yes*: heading out to meet whatever may be coming with an already-extended arm—as if ready to shake hands with a promising, heartening, equally glad future.

Ampelmann's history, easily found online, likewise moves and inspires. How on God's earth these stouthearted emblems made their debut in the starved, brutally guarded, beaten-down wasteland of a German Democratic Republic, is tough to imagine. Perhaps the little traffic light men served in some tiny way as encouragement. (Unthinkable hardship and cruelty were givens. Read Joel Agee's immortal memoir, *Twelve Years*, a record of his childhood as his then family struggled to survive in that Dante-esque netherworld.)

A shameless industry of tokens and goods has burst from these now-beloved images, from key chains to earrings, T-shirts to beach totes. It's an exploitation I can't begrudge. Even thinking about green Ampelmann, his sprightly, roving manner—easy to imagine him to be whistling—never fails to lift me, a sturdy cocktail of relief and hope. I've pasted a circular bumper sticker bearing his spry, stepping-out form on my car's back fender. And every time I lay eyes upon that sane, chipper, striding-toward-excellent-adventure fellow—something in me recalibrates. On the spot I resolve, willy-nilly, to do better, be better.

Only once—in the area near the river called Museum Island, where the city's most splendid museums align like a set of Parthenons—did a shadow fall over our spazz-out. A busker implored us in winsome sign language for contributions to an apparent charity for the deaf, putting his cheek to mine as a warrant of tender affection. I gave him a couple of euros. The busker had counted on receiving more than that. In an instant his Peter Pan charm vanished; contempt deadened his face as he turned away. He stalked off to count the afternoon's take with a female busker. I stared after them, embarrassed and angry with myself as much as with him— I'd been an idiot to fall, even a little, for his false bonhomie, and what was probably a total con anyway to fetch themselves cigarette and beer money. But what right had I to ordain some candy shell of unilateral cheer as the personality profile for an entire population—a population doubtless as needy and diverse and complicatedly fucked up as any other?

In hindsight, I missed certain cues—a tightness on people's faces and in their carriage, the ways they moved, spoke, stood. As noted earlier (against my own spazz-out's sugarcoating), I seldom felt from German people what you'd call innate warmth. The vibe was trickier. You might call it a kind of *girdedness*: a controlled, systematic tension of readiness-against-whatever-might-drop; getting on with duties while taking generic care not to cause harm. The message I absorbed from individuals we watched or with whom we had any transaction was *I do what I must.* In short, they were earning a living, taking care of life and business. Of course that's how people everywhere talk to themselves about hauling themselves to a job every day and performing, hour by hour, what that work requires. Perhaps the tightness I read was my own projection.

But surfaces can mislead, or at least rarely tell the whole story. Some months after we returned home, two *New Yorker* articles appeared. One, by historian Thomas Meaney, focused upon the alarming ascent in Germany of a neo-right-wing movement that tended to scapegoat immigrants. This piece gave the lie—unnervingly—to my breezy supposition that the country had once-and-for-all morphed into a model of humanitarianism by dint of sheer group will. The other article, by *New Yorker* staff writer Burkhard Bilger, was called "Ghost Stories." Bilger journeyed to Berlin to participate in a kind of progressive group therapy, designed to help middle-aged Germans ("unaccustomed to self-pity and allergic to national pride") exorcize the abiding internal pain of connection with all the history I'd so blithely assumed them safely past. "Theirs was a country responsible for history's bloodiest war and most efficient mass murder: sixty million killed, including two-thirds of all European Jews," writes Bilger. "They were here [in the therapy session] to wrestle with that guilt."

Grown children of German émigrés have not, it appears, escaped the same stigma. "Family history," Bilger notes, "is an uneasy topic for a German-American. . . . A sense of guilt by association hangs in the air, even for people of my generation." Bilger was born in 1964. "To be German, it seems, is still to be one part Nazi." As survivors with direct memories of the war are now dying off, "people began to realize how little they knew about their parents' and grandparents' lives. They needed to hear those terrible old stories after all . . . *Kriegskinder*, they called themselves: children of war." You need to know the story, it seems, to excise the story, to free yourself. "Evidence that the effects of trauma can reverberate through generations has steadily mounted," observes Bilger. He then recounts the anguish of each therapy group's participants, as they tried to understand the behavior of a family member who'd been involved on any level with Nazi actions.

Things had never, apparently, been what they seemed.

In truth, one real trauma did occur in Berlin—the only one of our voyage. Some people might reject that it qualifies as trauma. We weren't robbed or beaten; not blindsided by a car or a motorbike. No one was injured—mortally. The ordeal was interior: a private bomb whose latent power I'd been striving to escape, or bury deeper, with the busyness of travel.

It had nothing to do with Germany. Yet Germany was its context; therefore, its midwife.

It, too, happened at Museum Island, when I suddenly discovered I'd lost my special museum pass, purchased and handed to me by my husband only moments before—a pass good in all the museums for three days. We had just two days left in the city. Each pass cost about forty dollars, not a fortune but not nothing, and we were trying, as always, to control expenses. In the swirl of people pushing through the receiving area of our first museum— as we were puzzling out how to stash our belongings in one of those little lockers requiring a euro coin deposited in a sticky slot—my ticket disappeared. We later guessed I'd unwittingly dropped it, and that someone had scooped it. Next came a panicked fluster: furious checking of all pockets, dumping out of the handbag, followed by that frantic, sickened feeling when each object grasped and set aside is not the desired one nor is it sticking to, or hiding, the desired one. My husband—a good, sane, generous, consummately decent but mortal man—got angry with me, incredulous that within mere minutes of its purchase I could somehow have managed to let that pass evanesce into air.

In a stroke, I felt crushed.

Defeated. Emptied. Stupid—not fit to live; suddenly not much caring whether I lived.

Please now allow for a last, perhaps outrageously late disclosure, introducing the submerged monster in this odyssey—of personal grief.

My beloved younger sister, Andrea, had died, suddenly and horribly, of apparent pancreatic failure, about a year earlier. The event could not have been more abrupt—a bolt flung by a Greek god. And though my husband and I had eventually resumed life and travel, moving over the surface of the world in customary ways, I secretly felt as though I had to work twice as hard to convince myself (let alone others) that a world without her—lifelong copilot, witness, simultaneous mother and daughter, cosurvivor of multiple early losses—was still making sense as a world. Not least, I struggled to convince myself that whatever it was that I called "I" was still making sense as a part of that world. Until the moment of the vanished ticket, the world we looked upon had been making a reasonable show of worldness—if never quite fitting together as it once had.

To be sure, ghost reminders had whispered behind people, settings, objects. The names etched into the glass booth in Mannheim. The aloof, aging man whose roses she'd have praised. The babies and dogs, tchotchkes and weather.

During the months after losing her, I would hold my head with both hands to keep it from breaking open. *My little girl, my baby wren, soft brown feathers for hair, sitting opposite me on the cool smooth concrete of our Arizona front porch, repeating my language lessons with eager, smiling, trusting brown eyes. Hamburger.* Hangaber. *Spaghetti.* Ba-sketti. *Yellow.* Lellow.

It is a deeply strange experience to travel after the death of someone as close to you as your own skin. You regress in ways to a blank slate, almost needing to relearn the most basic assumptions and practices of a modern society. You look around in bafflement at the colossal, intricate, bearing-down life of a world that has neither paused nor changed a jot; you gaze in wonder at the busy, rushed, full-tilt nonstopness of things. Until our hapless halt near the museum's banks of lockers, the world's surface—if thin, if whisper-plagued—had sort of "held." When the little ticket disappeared and my husband grew angry, that thin construct shivered, suddenly crosshatched with a million infinitesimal cracks. In the next moment, like a hurled glass globe, it fell to bits. And so did I.

I didn't care anymore where we were, what we did, or whether we had money. I wanted my baby sister back—my second heart, known to me in every pore since they first brought her home in a blanket, she who best knew my own heart and the hearts of her children and husbands and friends, who did everything in her power (sometimes beyond her power) to put her arms around the world, make it happy—the kindest, gentlest, most loving soul I'll ever know, the only one left who could corroborate everything that had happened to us (early deaths of parents and husbands;

wayfaring lives eventually made good). In the words of a friend, "a million others should have gone before her."

But you see, they had. They did.

So how do we measure loss? I stared in shock at her motionless form in the hospital room—we'd arrived too late, too late—that adored face still frowning, as if in dismay and perplexion at the terrible pain that had been her last awareness, her last consciousness.

This really happened.

I have begged my little sister silently, every day since, to give me any sign that she still somehow, somewhere, *is*. No sign has come, except for dreams. They give the brief comfort of her presence, which may be all I or anyone can realistically hope for. Staring from my emptied handbag to my exasperated husband in the midst of that museum lobby's noisy mobs, I wanted only to slip back into one of those dreams, away from the brittle, thousand-arrows-deluge of living, to hold my sister tight, smell her clean, apricot-shampoo scent. Nothing mattered then. Not travel, not art, not food or drink, not even my dear husband. Not Germany, not planet Earth.

My husband, recognizing what had been loosed, scrambled to stanch and smooth it over—but I'd lost my bearings. Zombified, tear-streaked, I stumbled back to the ticket cage and bought another pass. We entered the museum. It was the Pergamon, I think. Gallantly, my husband (now in triage mode) tried to distract me, pointing out extraordinariness and sublimity in all directions. I could not respond—could not muster a straw of coherent thought, only sickened freefall as I cast my eyes toward magnificent pillars and priceless tapestries, jewelry, glassware, mosaics, weaponry, tools: marvelous things that people (now dust) had bravely made. I can still feel the bottomless cold abyss of it, the outer-space shriek in my ears. What good to me, the riches of ages? She was gone. What good was anything? What could, in fact, any longer be called good?

To whom, wailed one ancient Egyptian inscription, *can I speak today?*

My husband and I zigzagged, at careful distance from one

another, through immense rooms. The Germans, to their unend-
ing credit, had arranged sarcophagi, statuary, bas-reliefs, and
sculptured busts so that there was plenty of light-filled space
around each piece—each piece lit so artfully and subtly, the
works themselves seemed to glow. I tried to hang back, give my
husband a long lead, make room between us to allow for my ballooning horror, which I could not seem to control.

Here's a fact I can offer with authority: it is very hard to find
places in a museum's rooms where you can cry in privacy. Corners
seem to work best, if you face into them. Crave as I did to disap-
pear, the thing that is me lurched on in its same, mute, faithful
body: carrying case for a wailing soul.

We kept walking. (He walked. I trailed him.) At last we entered
a room in which a massive screen had been mounted on a base of
console height. A long bench was fixed at perfect viewing distance
across from the screen.

People were seating themselves there, to watch.

A sign above the installation promised simply, *Time Travel*.

We sat.

Then all at once we were seeing a semi-animated, computer
graphics–aided film, panning over a landscape of primitive Earth:
cave-dweller years, wintry and raw. Soon, swiftly, the camera
homed in on a family going about its then-life: a hefty fire crackling, animal skins drying. Details were visible. Our eyes were
guided over tools and implements, weapons and eating utensils,
crude clothing. Yet the quality of animation softened the view, the
panning camera almost smearing it so that the images came at us
like a sequence of half-remembered dreams. Then, above the
screen, a sort of chronometer (time-ometer?) fast-forwarded several
thousand years. And before we knew it we were watching a small
tribe building shelters, fishing, dancing, eating. Little kids scrambled; mothers called to them. Laughter. Hammering. Then the
time-ometer pushed ahead again and we watched two villages, or
townships, at war. We heard shouts and cries and horses screaming, clanks and clunks of metal and wood. A series of stills showed

men struggling in combat; we heard them howl in anger and pain. Eerily, what separated this cinematic dream from other kinds were its sounds. No specific language was ever clear but voices carried, voices like ours—as did the warmly familiar sounds of wind and weather, of animals, human merriment, human anguish, human sorrow.

We watched an early wedding. A funeral.

No single word was intelligible—only universally understood sounds.

This really happened.

Slowly my heart and body calmed and gentled.

Wordlessly, body and heart were absorbing some deep, cellular recognition: the continuum of human struggle, of atrocity, joy, agony and wonder, understood across incomprehensible spans of years.

Up floated a phrase I've never forgotten—the hand-lettered title of a folksy mineral display we'd browsed in the Arizona outback many years ago:

The vastness of geologic time.

And the whole of my tired, grieving body recalled slowly, as if by granules through an hourglass, that we had always been part of all we were viewing. Nothing more nor less. We were them. We would fade as they had, this long line of forebears. The time-ometer showed generations blurring inexorably back into a ceaseless, mostly forgotten past. Me, my sister, her children, their children. All of us sharing a fate stretched along an infinite continuum.

At last, in a trance, we rose and left the museum; emerged blinking into the dusk-lit city of Berlin, the country called Germany, the continent known as Europe, the planet named Earth, the year denoted, for reasons now nearly forgotten, by the number 2016. And in sepia light, overlooking wide streams of bellowing cars and buses, cop's whistles, hordes from everywhere moving across squares and playing music and drinking beer and romping with kids in parks and along the river in tour boats, monstrous building cranes nosed slowly side to side in the background as if nodding along with the human roar, against early evening's fading sun. People were moving, as they must. We moved with them, waking yet still entranced, striding out into it with intensifying resolve to do, to be. Among them, amid it. Heading out—why not—like Ampelmänchen to meet whatever might next come, while we could. All that is given to us to invent, to deploy, is response. Later I would think about the curious weightlessness of those moments as we joined the surging cars and crowds—but also about how, at the same time, I felt the time-ometer pressing forward: infinitesimal, patient, relentless. And in truth it was not a bad feeling, not bad at all.

Place as Answer

HGTV

On the road, my husband and I binge-watch the Home and Garden Network.

So what? Innocent as a taste for popcorn, you may say. But consider: the habit signifies.

Mightily.

My husband likes to think about real estate. Both of us like to think about homes—abstract and literal—though, counterintuitively, we never watch HGTV in our own house. Maybe the threat of humiliation-by-comparison is too great.

Maybe distance allows more objectivity. Or more room to dream.

Oddly, HGTV seldom utters the actual words *real estate*. Possibly the term unnerves people with its sleazy pomp. (During the years I lived in Hawaii, the words *real estate agent* automatically meant *someone-not-necessarily-very-bright, on the make.* Why else would you be selling off pieces of a finite, incalculable treasure to anyone, just because they could pay for it?)

(Mainland realtors, alas, don't often present much differently. There's just more to sell.)

The words still evoke dueling images: that of an aftershave-soaked hustler thrusting a bogus contract at you for, say, time-shares in a Florida swamp—versus the painterly view of the wide, virginal earth, the hard (or yielding) soil or sand or rock beneath your feet. Something is at once noble and wretched about the burden and gift of property: exalting and damning, Pearl Buck and Scarlett O'Hara, scrabbling for potatoes in the stubborn dirt and shaking one's fist at the sky one moment, the next beaming in contentment, to an Aaron Copland soundtrack, as lord of all one surveys.

Just the word *estate* suggests vast, splendid acreage like what we imagine Russian aristocracy owned, but also what history repeatedly tells us was bought and stolen and worked with blood and sweat: a solemn prize guarded and hoarded, coveted and squandered, passed along by legacy like family jewels. Modern idiom calls whatever structure we inhabit *space*, since in urban settings it occurs many stories above the ground. What matters is that the space is provably, legally ours.

Then we can fixate on what to do with it.

Once installed in our motel room, done with the day's navigating, my husband busies himself finding the HGTV channel while I assemble the wine and beer, the crackers and nuts. Even if we're tired, looking forward to these shows makes us cheerful. They cost nothing. They won't give me bad dreams (something I'm prone to). They function as a sort of dimwit's travelogue, flashing glimpses of parts of the world we may not yet have seen—or that we might contrast with our own experience of them (Mississippi, Costa Rica, a Greek island). Watching HGTV's supersimplified plots and vanilla settings, its fast-forward progress (labor performed off-camera between takes by low-paid grunts) makes us laugh, but also vexes and stimulates us, igniting great gusts of opinion—usually shouted.

Yet the above doesn't explain the riddle of HGTV's intense appeal. What, at heart, is its lure? Why do people who know better watch this? Why do these shows hypnotize us?

My husband and I don't fit the channel's target demographic. We don't care about buying stuff. In fact we *hate* buying stuff—that is, things. (We would rather spend money on cheap travel.) We drive old, compact cars and live in a paid-off 1930s bungalow he bought thirty years ago—before house prices in our Northern

California county went stratospheric, making buying a house impossible for the young, and a spectator sport for all but the uber-wealthy. Our little house has charm but it's saggy and worn; like many others of its kind, it makes no sense in terms of its formal appraisal value. It's a funky house in a neighborhood that lately—as a bedroom to tech zillionaires working in San Francisco—has become desirable. We are proud of our digs, a hair defensive, a hair embarrassed. I call our kitchen a miniversion of the kitchen in Monet's shambly Giverny house. *Shabby chic* is our only-half-joking motto.

Yet HGTV tugs at something in us—at something in most everyone. People of all stripes crave an idea of Home—the whole cantilevered fantasy, its intricate particulars whirling and fanning, a vision the world can never stop parsing. In English, the word *home* contains the meditative OM sound, a sustained vibration that seems to inject our bones with an irresistible promise—sanctuary, safety, peace, freedom—and together with those notions, *all the feels*, as social media puts it. Ease, serenity, security. The right fit. Belonging.

Sounds like biblical absolution, doesn't it? Heavenly balm. The ideal home will bring us into focus; make us whole, well, clear. Our best selves will bloom—as if tapped by a magic wand—because of where we happen to stand upon the planet and (not least) in what sort of shelter: the pile, the base, the HQ where we eat and sleep and bathe, dream and cry, love and brood and laugh; in some places, echoing earlier eras, where we're born and die.

Is it any wonder we never stop looking, analyzing, comparing—even if we believe we already love where we live? It seems that whatever container wraps our bodies—mansion, shed, ricksha, cardboard box—the idea of home gives off a pheromone that never stops seducing us; never stops hinting that it will answer for all time (for our lifetimes, at least) an ancient question.

Where you are means who you are.

HGTV simplifies and stylizes. Story lines follow an old, cherished arc: Joseph and Mary search for an inn. But unlike the biblical characters, HGTV clients aren't turned away; that house or apartment will be sold or rented to Joseph and Mary. A fairy-tale flavor also infuses these carefully paid-out story lines: the starring couple tours three sites, expected to choose one. Never mind that dozens were considered and eliminated off-camera, or that the decision took place long before the filmed "aha." Part of each plot's (very gentle) tension involves trying to guess which place each couple will choose, given what we've been primed to understand of their personalities, needs, and budgets.

Unsurprisingly, each couple, like each home, matches a template or blueprint. Generally, Joseph and Mary are heterosexual (though the shows occasionally host same-sex couples and also, thank God, interracial pairs). They are youngish, married, sometimes pregnant. Sometimes they already have a kid or two or four. Often they are starting out, not married. (I guess that's attitudinal progress: Wikipedia says HGTV is headquartered in Knoxville, Tennessee.) They often have jobs that sound suspiciously vague: web-presence development or investment consulting. We listen closely for mentions of these jobs, because we want to guess how much these people earn—the better to grasp how Joseph and Mary will be able to finance the project at hand.

Sometimes we aren't allowed to know how people afford it. One couple had a budget of several million. They weren't volunteering how they came by it, and no one was asking. They wound up buying a mansion in the desert hills that featured a Viking-sized dining hall and a separate, long barroom, with actual saddles fixed to the tops of each barstool as seats. That's the kind of detail that makes us laugh—partly with relief not to be anywhere near those people.

Sometimes, especially outside the US, the project at hand means simply finding an apartment to rent. But here, a house will be found. That's one kind of HGTV show.

Others showcase a chosen home's whopping makeover.

Extremely important to the American home-makeover narrative are three phases: Before, After, and—for the sake of dramatic tension—Monkeywrench in the Middle, meaning the sudden, midway discovery of unforeseen, nasty obstacles. Termites or mold or vermin have infested the structure. A root system has destroyed part of the foundation. Pipes or beams have rotted, or some ghastly toxin needs to be removed. Whatever the snag, it will cost serious money to fix, and it threatens to cripple the project. The couple is filmed in close-up, turning to each other in these "crisis" moments. I assume viewers are supposed to be titillated by the suffering the couple endures, trying to reach a decision. (Suffering is an essential feature of reality television, something that troubles me deeply, though maybe it's just a cruder manifestation of theatrical art—but that's another discussion.)

Pressure, in any case, is on. We've been told (several times) the amount of the couple's budget. And though we know plain as day that these hardies will overcome their trials—otherwise there'd be no show, correct?—we viewers can't help worry, or at least be breathlessly caught up. We're human, and what's at stake is a home (that ripe, reverberating word) that is supposed to become these people's Valhalla, their *heimat*, their fortress where they may safely gather, be loved and protected and nourished: their best versions of themselves.

It stiffens me a little to think about how (and where and by whom) these narratives are plotted—the same way you'd rather not see sausages being made. But the boilerplate model—an act of storytelling, after all—nails its objectives every time. It draws attention, provokes desire (creates desire), and, yes, sells product—whatever the show's commercials are peddling, cheese spread or varnish or air freshener. If they did not sell product, the shows—the whole network—would be canceled. Simple as that. Numbers rule. Cruel, yes, but so are life and capitalism. (Not that I'm seeing any brilliant alternatives to either out there.)

Our attention spans are short. And alongside a pitiless bottom line (does the show make money or not), writers and producers understand short attention spans. First and last, it's the emotion of home-finding and homemaking that ropes in viewers and, consequently, sells product. That's the channel's great paradox: emotion makes money. Except maybe that's how marketing has worked since the beginning of time. Sell the sizzle.

I like the *Property Brothers*, who latterly appear to be attaining rock-star status: nice-looking twins Drew and Jonathan Scott, now in their early forties. They may act smug on camera—both of them sporting sly, wry, just-ate-the-canary smiles—but they also come across as funny, cheerful, and knowledgeable. They seem to make clients happy. At the time of this writing, another program, *Fixer Upper*, starred Chip and Joanna Gaines, a handsome Texas couple (five kids by the time the series ended) who renovated homes for people of different backgrounds and means. They, too, seemed to make clients happy, and this in turn seemed genuinely to make them happy (to whatever degree we can consider anything on television to be genuine). In still another show, an attractive couple (attractiveness a requirement) specializes in restoring disintegrating old homes in a mopey southeastern town to help that (crumbling, ignored) little burg apply a fresh face, attract new residents, and clamber back into respectable life. And there's a program that specializes in house-and-apartment-hunting for people all over the world, using the enticing *bing-bong* of a doorbell as its theme sound.

These formats, and others like them, pulse with near-pornographic magnetism. It's hard to pull your gaze away. You can't help notice the lurid bits zoomed in upon: the dank cellar; the aging bathroom sinks; the outmoded, rusting fixtures, water stains, cracks, insect infestations, rot, and so on. Inevitably, we're shown the subject couple (two women, last time I tuned in) sitting down together with glasses of wine to talk things over. At the end—strictly essential—comes the payoff, popularly known as the Big Reveal (and whoever coined that prototypically American, flat-footed term should either be shot or commemorated, or both). We're staring finally at the remade house: fresh, flawless new rooms, hardwood floors, walls, fixtures, lawns. It's been staged with perfect furniture, tasteful art, carpets, luminous window shades, bowls of oranges—the works. This is when anyone's heart may dimple with envy. New, clean surfaces! (Doubtless it smells like a million bucks.) Spaciousness! Never mind the furnishings may be on loan, returned to the sponsors after filming and replaced by *Grapes of Wrath* relics—or by nothing at all. We who live in old houses are susceptible to the gleam factor.

We can even experience the envy without sound. In my gym's cardio room, sweaty strivers easily follow HGTV on televisions mounted above our ellipticals, treadmills, and stationary bikes. In fact the drama is more readable without sound: wary, big-eyed clients looking like a couple of baby lambs in a used car lot, as the Property Brothers or similar cute, suave shepherds move in swiftly to herd them along.

What touches me about the channel's appeal is our indestructible hunger for newness, remaking, fresh starts, reinvention—all our optimism harnessed in pursuit of a new dream—and how we decide, at the same time, what elements constitute that dream. As the luscious visuals, itemized wish lists (with check marks), and commercials roll across the screen, an observant space alien dropping through could easily get clues about what American earthlings call a desirable home. A thinking American earthling, on the other hand, can't not, eventually, feel uneasy about it. Why? Because of the staggering amount of our one-life-only, waking energies marshaled toward the next transformation, busily dragging what we consider ideal into what's real, manifesting what we passionately believe will answer everything and somehow completely satisfy us—guaranteeing us a quality of days and hours that redeem life on earth.

Nothing more, nor less.

I have mused, occasionally, about how blissful it might be to live in a world of commercials.

Commercials tell us the story of what to want and how to get it. They are populated by beautiful humans savoring the Gotten Thing in comfort and joy. Advertising enacts our desires while reminding us to desire: pillows to peanut butter, antidepressants to constipation remedies. People act kind, friendly, jubilant. They're beyond satisfied—they're ecstatic. Everyone loves everyone, and would like to buy the world a Coke. Commercials don't hesitate to answer that second-most ancient question (second after where home is), which art also struggles, in all its warty clumsiness, to answer:

How, then, should we live?

I don't know why it never occurred to me before.

The entire HGTV network is—of course—one gigantic commercial.

And I'm obliged to confess, at the same time, that something powerfully weird happens after you've taken in too much HGTV. You feel a little sick, as if you'd eaten a bowl of stale icing. If everything is purely sweet and all-at-the-surface, all the time—which HGTV hornswoggles even the best of us (for a while) into imagining—we begin to feel rocky.

Something so big is missing, we can't—choking on sweetness-sickness—even name it.

When my husband and I travel, I often study homes and apartment complexes we pass—who does not do this?—absorbing as much of what I see as I can, wondering who lives inside; what kinds of lives they are having.

HGTV suggests that it's showing us exactly that: who lives there, and what kinds of lives they—we—are having.

Wickedly, I can't help fantasize a follow-up program: a reality check series (RCTV), a late-night chaser fashioned in the mode of *Where Are They Now?* that systematically goes around revisiting all those couples and families we saw joyfully installed in their respective, perfect homes—say five years after they've moved in. The ones who gasped and wept and clapped their hands, who stared at the snow-pure walls and cannily chic furniture and sparkling bathrooms with awe—watching their dream come true so they might begin, at last, to live that dream.

I can't help wonder what happened next.

Then I wonder why I wonder that.

But I already know why, somewhere beneath my ribs. It's because I suspect that nothing gold can stay. Is this schadenfreude? Is it jealousy? Or is it a melancholy facing-off with some irrefutable human penchant? We could make the case that choosing a home is like a choosing a spouse, and we've all repeatedly been told how bad the survival odds for marriages are, at least in the United States. But that analogy would be too pat, too broad. My sense is that a dwelling has no opinions. It doesn't elect to fail or betray or offend us; doesn't fall prey to unwholesome temptations. A house doesn't choose to let its allegiances drift, become restless or intractable, or gleefully turn a knife in our guts.

Those events, for whatever reasons, spring straight from us, from within ourselves. A home is vulnerable to weather, nature, and our whims.

What may have seemed The Answer not that long ago becomes, complicatedly or simply, not so much wrong as outmoded, off the mark, insufficient.

It's as if Desire itself were exerting its supremacy over and over, crowning itself the winner no matter what the reward.

A New Answer is again wanted. The search resumes. And who knows? Perhaps the search will yet again be televised, for viewers to admire, identify with, dream about.

Rules for the Well-Intended

Some months ago, a close family member planned an extended trip to Europe—by himself—for the first time. My relative, while superbly accomplished in his profession, has lived alone for decades, is gaining in years, and had never traveled anywhere before, to speak of, exempting a ball game in a nearby city.

I grew worried.

I decided to set down a few basic pointers for him before he left. I knew I risked sounding like a meddler or a prude, maybe paranoid, even a scold. But the thought of him shuffling along with his worn backpack and baggy surf shorts and huaraches, radiating naïveté, unpredisposed (putting it gently) to assess the scene or think twice about much of anything—I feared he may as well have been wearing a sandwich board that shouted *rob me.*

The few guidelines I felt compelled to offer would be, I hoped, self-explanatory.

But the words I sent him, after I'd stared at them awhile, made me sad and self-conscious. They sounded brittle, fearful, withholding. Those words did result, however, from experience, and must be classified—however unhappily—as common sense. When we think about travel, it serves nothing to deny certain realities. Even the emperor of travel, Rick Steves, was pickpocketed—in Paris no less, where he (above all others) should have known better. That fact, together with Steves's willingness to admit his gaffe (foolishly keeping his wallet in his back pocket) also made me sad.

This thinking led me back (in a well-worn confrontational loop) to the riddle of why we travel at all.

Steves is adamant on the subject, writing frequently and energetically about it. *Keep on travelin'!* is his robust motto, a cheerful cheek-pinch-and-salute with which he grinningly closes each videotaped episode. Steves continues doing his utmost to spread the gospel of travel for travel's sake, explaining (on television, in blogs and interviews) that he believes travel can only help us become more aware of each other as world citizens—help us see ourselves in one another, and therefore (the tacit reasoning extends) not be as prone to hate and destroy each other. An earlier trope for this thinking, meant to avert nuclear disaster with the then–Soviet Union by means of personal visitor exchanges, was called Track Two Diplomacy.

But besides generic distraction, cultural novelty, and the above, shining ideal of good will, why bother? What's the point? Elsewhere I have speculated that a possible answer may be the refrain from the old drinking song "The Bear Went Over the Mountain":

"To see what we can see."

But one chips away at this question from a range of angles.

I asked an older, wiser friend. Part of her answer: "A chance to float in anonymity and silence and wonder."

She thought it useful to issue a few rules, too. Hers went as follows:

- Never think you understand anything about the country. Accept being only a tourist.
- Make no generalizations about the culture and the people, but always try to be a kind and humble guest in their country.
- Understand that you come from a country where physical comfort and privilege have been, until recently, more extensive for more middle-class types, and have come (until recently) at less cost.
- Know when the weather has licked you.

These strike me as gentle and reasonable (and with the weather part, somewhat funny). But to me they don't face down enough grit. Until some kind of revolution changes things (which none of us should ever rule out), American travelers do tend to live better than most of the world—and most of the world, along its various corridors of transit, is desperately on the take.

Forced to be on the take, you might even say.

Haves and Have Nots. Supply and Demand. Everyone has many stories.

Here were the seasoned traveler's ground-floor commandments I sent to my relative:

- *Passport, wallet, phone*: the eternal mantra. Kept on your body at almost all times (passport can be stowed in a secure hotel room or hotel safe—for men, nothing in back pockets). Clap a hand over each article while you murmur that mantra, every single day (maybe every hour) before making a move or setting off for anywhere. Feel the fact of them.
- Never let go of your belongings. Maintain sharp awareness of where you are, where your stuff is, who is around you, how the immediate vibe feels. Do not be charmed by anyone who strikes up conversation. This doesn't mean being a paranoid jerk; it does mean keeping a force field of alert space around you.
- Do not "hold" anything for anyone who approaches with that request. Extract yourself at once from groups (including little kids) who crowd up and start asking questions or pawing at you. Teenagers on public transport have a trick: one young person asks you innocent, beguiling questions as another expertly picks your pocket or motionlessly unzips your handbag or pack while you are concentrating on answering your enchanting questioner. This happened to me on the Paris metro (the teens were interrupted by the shriek of a nearby,

simultaneous victim; they were obliged to race off without my wallet).

- If something wet or fruity suddenly splatters you in the back or on your head or shoulder, do not stop in confusion but keep walking faster—and at once push away and flee anyone who (instantly) appears to "wipe you off." This is, I'm so sorry to say, another pickpocketing ploy, and tends to happen very quickly. It happened to a dear friend and her husband their first day in a South American city. They had to spend the next several days canceling credit cards, applying for replacement identification, and so forth.

- Finally, at the risk of sounding drearily obvious: do not count or handle your cash or examine credit cards or phone in public view. (A friend's phone was snatched from his hand while he was staring at it—this, too, in Paris. The thieves ran. He gave chase, but was unable to catch them.) Before using an ATM be aware of who's around: if it feels or looks sketchy, it probably is; find a better locale, preferably one inside the bank or its portico. Do not get drawn into seemingly friendly theatrics. Put cash away rapidly.

On the kinder, brighter side of these advisories, I'd add simply: Stay curious. (This actually also means taking adequate rest and nourishment to feel well enough to care.) Attend and retain as much of the avalanche of "so various, so beautiful, so new" as possible.

My relative did not, as it turned out, do badly with these rules. He learned plenty. (That his favorite sugarless gum might not be automatically available in mom-and-pop grocers. That ice is insanely hard to obtain. That Wi-Fi service flickers and wobbles in and out. That most cities feature terrific art museums filled with mind-boggling treasures. That excellent live music happens routinely in subways, parks, cafes. That most food, up and down the price-point ladder, is damn good. That it's best to keep your pulled carry-on snugged close to your heels lest you trip some luckless human walking in its path. That public transport is doable, and gives great views.) Overall, he enjoyed his odyssey. He was not mugged or conned. He did get sick toward the end of his adventures, with some violent intestinal ordeal—but that's a pitfall not always easy to thwart.

First and last, *messieurs-dames*: we are obliged, for our parts, not to be jackasses.

Obliged by what, you ask? By common decency, which—sadly—is not always common. By which I mean: too often decency is most starkly missing—more sadness—among Americans.

I've told my husband that I can tell who's American in an overseas public setting before they open their mouths (and when the mouths open, last scraps of doubt are removed). Americans of all ages tend to be bigger—visibly better fed—than most, and as a partnering feature, louder. Cockier. More dramatically gestural—often rudely so. I am frequently embarrassed by my countrymen and -women in foreign lands. They tend to be obnoxious, demanding, and oblivious; to ignore cultural cues and behave as if they owned everything around them, expecting citizens of their host country to render precise services in perfect English. They act out at top volume in places that obviously prize quiet, courtesy, calm—again, where English is not the preponderant language. I am fairly sure these herds of Americans (at least those who may think twice about it, which would not be many) believe themselves not only to be savvy iconoclasts but that they are actually doing the surrounding, benighted natives a *favor*; teaching them better, livelier, more interesting ways to carry on. What's missing in most cases is any sensitivity to the setting—in short, bare-bones respect. We've watched people assuming jokey poses as they snap photos of each other in front of the remnants of the Berlin Wall.

What also becomes cringe-makingly clear when I witness my fellow citizens being idiots is the reconfigured perception of locals; of passers-by or serving personnel who must deal with recurring hordes of vulgar visitors. Inevitably, their faces reflect a kind of willed endurance: profound weariness, redoubled efforts to complete tasks with patience and dignity, and infiltrating all that, a visible mixture of pity, incredulity, and scorn.

My husband swears it's his experience that each traveling citizen is most embarrassed by his or her own countrymen in a foreign setting, no matter where they're from: the Danes are fretful about the cluelessness of traveling Danes, the English about the obtuseness of the touring English, and so on. I am touched by the democracy of his concept, and semipersuaded that some of it may sometimes prove true—but not convinced. Without naming names, I can admit that there are several countries besides the United States whose denizens have graphically earned an international reputation for being public louts. But I strongly suspect that Americans lead the charge of that awful brigade.

Why are they—why are we—that way? Because the portion of us able to afford international travel—and willing to take on the modicum of risk it will involve—has (nonetheless) grown accustomed to getting exactly what we want when we want it, in English and dollars, thank you very much. And we assume that the ability to pay for it justifies everything: that is, after all, the tacit American creed.

One can't change those for whom one feels semi-responsible (by association), therefore ashamed.

One can do one's best, by example, to *offset* them.

What, you may wonder, might be my private rules for myself, during travel—besides those cited for my relative?

They would be something along the lines of my older friend's:

Take everything in, humbly, warily, thoughtfully. Shut up. Whenever possible, defer. Assume little. Let experience marinate. Much later, try to reassemble and reinterrogate the memories. And only then, perhaps, begin—begin!—to find out what you may think.

Think of England

1.

As a child I often sat alone at day's end, to think. I parked my bottom on the warm top step of our front porch in Sunnyslope, Arizona—a dusty little postwar outpost, seed of a suburb, dozing at the feet of the gentle North Phoenix mountains. The town's first, crude roads—many unpaved— wound around the bases of the desert hills as if finger-drawn. Our tract's tiny houses, bravely new after World War II, were a first-time owner's pride; you could still smell raw lumber and fresh paint.

I loved the desert. I loved my known life there.

Elbows on knees, chin propped in fisted hands, I'd watch the sun drop behind the houses opposite me: sky turning scarlet-pink, then pewter, then cobalt.

I'd feel the air cool, see a cloud of midges zip and zag, and consider what I knew so far. And during one such session I clearly remember registering this:

The world is very big. But whomever I end up with will have to be American.

Children think such things.

The silence around me in those hours felt eternal. So did time. Most everything feels eternal when you're a kid. I assumed time, back then, to be *the* great mystery. Still do. Where or what was I before I was born? Where or what would I be after I died? (Was I really going to *die*?) Where were the boundaries, the starting line and finish line of the infinite universe, the edges of time? What existed outside those boundaries? What then bounded that? (How could the infinite have boundaries?)

Kids think that stuff, too. More than anyone imagines; more than they let on.

I understood, from all accounts, that time would (glacially) pass. I knew that some faraway day I'd grow up and meet someone. I knew (from trick-or-treating for UNICEF) that different kinds of people, including kids like me, lived in varying circumstances all over the globe. And somehow—with zero experience—I sensed it would be tough to make a grown-up life with someone born outside American culture.

How such an awareness spoke to me then, or why, I still can't guess.

Even as I lengthened and (one hopes) deepened into adulthood—even after time spent in Peace Corps West Africa, where some of my co-volunteers wound up marrying Senegalese citizens; even after travel with a (part-Hawaiian) boyfriend to the UK and Europe for our first, electrifying views of the Old World—despite all my *Family of Man* upbringing and orientation, I never changed my childhood idea. I couldn't imagine living with someone who did not own a genetic grasp of the idiosyncratic (crazy) habits and speech of American culture, for better or worse. That grasp would have to be, to my thinking, primal.

Please know this never meant I felt superior about American history. My hunch, even so young, was practical. I assumed (even then) that it would cost too much, metaphysically—stress, blame, judgment, guilt—to have to explain each tic and gesture, to have to constantly translate (for a still-unmet, maybe nonexistent mate), hurdle by hurdle, all the strange, errant, often horrific ways that Americans are, and have been.

The horrific of then was not the horrific of now, of course. Horrific then was more like a great scary haze bulging against the edges of thought, formless but imminent, hinting of everything one feared yet could not then understand: the existence of evil; the queasy power of inscrutable words like "communist;" what exactly sex involved, or even meant. Notions so creepily amorphous they escaped describability in the mind of a child.

But explaining American life to a foreign mate? Where would one start? Sheerest pronunciation of the language alone might take years to convey, let alone defend.

2.

As I grew older, I entered a series of relationships with American men. Some were disastrous, some relatively pleasant. A few lasted long enough to be tantamount to marriages. None, finally, stuck. By age forty-three, living alone in San Francisco, I knew my odds for meeting a potential mate had probably all but disappeared. Most of the good men near my age, in that time and place, were married or gay.

I was trying to make peace with those facts when, pretty much by accident, reader, I fell in love with an Englishman.

Not just any Englishman: a Northerner. (Please now divide England into four planets: North, South, the Midlands, and London.) My husband was Northern by birth, rearing, and culture, until (by dint of his own gifts and drive) he attended Leicester University in the Midlands at age eighteen, which opened the world to him. He wound up traveling to California's Bay Area on a Fulbright scholarship to teach, where he stayed on. Later, after several dramatic relationships of his own, he met me.

Now, because I've mined huge portions of my wonderful husband's life for so (very) much other material, and because he has borne this mining for so long with such extraordinary patience and humor, I'll try to leave him out of this discussion—except to race to the punch line, by way of summary: after spending most of his adult life here he "gets" America, and Americans, better than fine. Better than me, sometimes. But his origins have allowed me to experience England in ways that many Americans never can. And it's Englishness in general, as I have sampled it, that I want to think about here.

3.

Most Americans in my orbit seem to view England in one of two ways: first, with a thin amusement, the way you'd glance at a quaint postcard or curiosity shop window. These Americans assume that the fabled mother country has, like an aging grandma, shrunk and wizened into some benign, mindless relic; a place semi-notable for dotty people, fussy habits, and archaic traditions. The other view is cow-eyed with touristic romance. These blissed-out souls picture all the highlights: changings of guards, Covent Garden, double-decker buses, red phone kiosks, besuited gentlemen with bowler hats marching smartly along Fleet Street or snapping open a newspaper from an armchair in a book-lined private club; ornate teas with clotted cream (why is clotted cream a good thing?), sausage rolls, foamy pints, and everywhere the sort of adorably clueless, bumbling bluster like that kicked up by Nigel Bruce (when he played Dr. Watson to Basil Rathbone's Sherlock Holmes). These Americans are charmed pantsless by what they perceive to be a British accent. (They make no distinctions among accents, often lumping them together.) They see the Royal Family as a kind of dollhouse they can peer into, assembling the cute little inhabitants and making them hop around the stale, gilded, heavily upholstered rooms of Buckingham Palace wearing adorable costumes. Most Americans don't know, don't remember, or avoid reminders of English history or traditions of Empire: enslavement, plunder, genocide, poverty, starvation, child labor, disease, debtors' prisons, and so forth. The closest many modern Americans come to acknowledging a grain of such unpleasantness might be when they recall the charcoal-smeared cheeks of the kid actors warbling "Who will buy" in the musical *Oliver!*—few now remember even that.

(Of course, we Americans are absolutely as unwilling to stare long at our own grisly pasts—our bloodstained land-grabbing and genocides. We're unwilling to stare long at anything. "Subject" is a shape-shifting, evasive commodity now—as is the real-time focus allocated to any subject at all. "Attention Deficit" may define our collective gaze.)

I should append now my respect, even awe, for the deep, far-reaching English intellectual tradition, for English literature particularly, which some claim eclipses everything else. In my own consciousness, this respect began not systematically with Shakespeare or Tudors or Victorians, not with Bloomsbury or Forster or Churchill (all those came later), but rather in blurts and blops, starting (improbably) in childhood with American airings of the plays of Harold Pinter (scary), and sneaky appearances on my home's shelves of works by Dickens, Kipling, eventually Kingsley Amis, Muriel Spark, and Virginia Woolf, Auden and Larkin; later the light brigade charge of Martin Amis, Julian Barnes, the late Christopher Hitchens, and Ian McEwen, later still of Margaret Drabble, Penelope Fitzgerald, A. S. Byatt; with films like *The Loneliness of the Long-Distance Runner* or *Women in Love* or, unforgettably, *King of Hearts*. Random bits arrived erratically as I was coming of age in the sixties.

That a slender margin of thoughtful American intellectuals have long paid homage to a (much fatter) margin of fearless English intellectuals—that they'd been doing so for a long time—registered faintly with me at first, more firmly later. But these realms seemed to exist at a blurred remove from popular culture on both sides of the Atlantic, which has probably (sadly) always been the relationship of a general populace to its thinkers and artists; even—perhaps especially?—in the country that has served since early centuries as home to Oxford and Cambridge.

4.

Nonetheless, visiting his family and friends in England (North and South) with my husband, interacting with them, observing them, and living for many years with his hardscrabble Northern memories and perspectives, taught me something over time that I don't think most uninitiated Americans ever truly grasp:

The rule of class. The saturating, ironfisted, determining fact of class.

Every feature of it—delegation, relegation, assumptions, expectations; the map it draws, the rules it enforces; the obdurate, arbitrary perqs and privileges, the embedded exclusions, doom, and damage—irradiates and drives English life, culture, and character, since forever. Full stop.

And yes, we Americans have class humbug. But I'm telling you—not like this.

I feel my head starting to ache already. There's no good or simple way to convey the depth, breadth, or relentlessness of it. What's more, a lot of people in my intimate orbit are going to be extremely unhappy to find these words, and I will likely be made to pay for it, probably in ways I can't yet fathom. I'll go ahead—with one important disclaimer.

I'm not an expert. Not a scholar nor specialist; not a student— not even a hobbyist of English life and culture, except by sporadic, sloppy habit. My education is a Swiss cheese: full of big holes.

Most glaringly, most damningly, I'm not a native.

No way to escape, nor deny, the fearful curse of this. My husband's late mother declared—to my face, with fairly un-English vehemence—"You don't understand the English, and you don't understand *me.*" Indeed. Her family (English, of course) and I (technically family but never, ever English) were trying to persuade her—at that point for her own safety—to consider moving into a light-filled, handsome, comfortably appointed, friendly, assisted-care community. She was having none of it.

I can only tell you what I've gathered after a number of visits and a chunk of years living with one of its Northern-born, postwar sons. (Sorrowfully, the greater part of two prior generations of England's sons were lost during both world wars.)

England is—oh, the limitless ways to finish that sentence. Myriad, maddening, endearing, infuriating, inscrutable, insoluble, intractable. Cozy, kind. Clipped, callous. Straitjacketing, pitiless. Strangulating. Cheery. Coarse. Chilly. Crisp. It can feel like what I think Churchill once called the Soviet bloc: a riddle wrapped in a mystery inside an enigma.

What's often vexing to me, again, is how many Americans fall like drugged puppies for the seemingly agreeable, droll, mannerly English surface. Judging from that surface, entire populations can entertain like an eccentric auntie, bustling or pottering, everybody a hail-fellow-well-met; the essence—the *exemplar*—of civilized. To some degree, this impression may at first feel like a haven of gentility, a fabulous reprieve from the violence and vulgarity we Americans routinely know. (One element does serve this way: not many guns over there. Imagine.) Brits can present as downright demure, if you don't count the occasional gang of drunken yobs (thugs) on the tube (underground subway). This surface perception can lull the innocent visitor. Only time and a handy interpreter let you understand that beneath the gracious, clever, self-disparaging wit lurks a complicated, rather stunningly ruthless, deep-end-of-the-iceberg. You begin to understand, over a long learning curve, that *forgive me for boring you* means not *silly me and my irrelevant, provincial concerns* but rather *I am repulsed by everything you stand for and I do not for one nanosecond take you seriously enough to be worth trusting with my actual thoughts. Be assured that you will never, ever know me because you are genetically incapable of that quality of perspicacity.*

Any questions?

It takes time for this comprehension to sink in, but once it does, the wary American zips up her instincts for any fresh-faced stepping forward, or for seeking meaningful exchange. Realizing one is being poked with a mockery stick pretty much murders any wish to "really know" the poker. That shift in awareness can briefly console, a kind of defiant dusting of hands: *Fine, too bad for you then.* But soon that response too becomes sort of irrelevant. Jennifer Schaffer has written a fine article for the *Paris Review* about marrying an Englishman and, as a witlessly earnest American, having to learn English ropes. Schaffer notes "'the upside-down language' Brits use to indicate approval ('that will do') and disdain ('she's *perfectly lovely'*), the paradoxical mix of socialized medicine and affordable education in a society that constantly emphasizes the importance of knowing—and sticking to—one's place."

And here's Julian Barnes on the subject: "We didn't do anger. . . . We did ironic comment, snappy rejoinder, satirical elaboration . . . [F]or anything beyond this, we did the thing enjoined upon the English middle classes for generations. We internalised our rage, our anger, our contempt." After a few rounds of receiving their courtly deflection-with-fangs-tucked-away, an American visitor enters any English social situation with fists up, determined to reveal nothing.

Soon, however, that stance becomes tedious, and she thinks: ah, to hell with it. Let the offenses fall where they may.

In fairness? They're like that with each other, too.

5.

Countryside, in a parallel way, can seduce, much of it stunning as any number of lovely old paintings. That's tricky for the same reasons English social silkenness is tricky. Because land, needless to say, is irrevocably connected with the sky over it—with weather. Which is bound, boomerang style, to circle back and slam.

Outside the blighted industrial sections, England can strike the newcomer (see above) as jaw-droppingly beautiful. My God, that green. I can't think of anything like it. Rich, cool, blue-infused. (That James Herriott book cover, with the patchwork of green fields bounded by low, evergreen-dark hedgerows? Realer than real.) Blue-saturated emerald, like the jewel-green illustrating fairy tales. Green to fill the eyes and soul, green to fuel poetry for millennia. It's a heavenly gift—especially to those of us born in arid lands; a green we'd otherwise never imagine.

It is that quality of green, of course, for an excellent reason.

It rains the holy living pitiless Christ-bitten bejesus out of that place.

Oh, how it rains. Dear *Lord*, but it rains. This news may, to the uninitiated, seem trivial. Nothing could be more wrong. Topography means climate. Climate shapes, infiltrates, and drives everything. All the world (interior and exterior) is generated and defined by it. Could *Wuthering Heights* or *Jude the Obscure* or *Whistle Down the Wind* have sprung from Southern California?

Sometimes, it rains year-round. "Summer" amounts to a *fond idea* in England. Yes, sometimes parts of the country get warm for a while, and on occasion—mark it well—hot. But these instances are diamonds in (damp, moldy) hay. When September arrives without a single moment's letup in three months of Ugly—of cold, windy, needling, sideways rain—people in the country grow, shall we say, very tight around the mouth. No one can think of anything upbeat to say, even in passing. I've seen grunts and eye-rolling, by way of greeting.

They know their last shot at even a facsimile of natural warmth has vanished. They'll soon be locked into Double Ugly—relentless, brittle, brutal winter—until God knows when.

Rain there is so constant and so varied, the country has devised (like fabled Arctic terms for snow) a centuries-honed range of language for it. Most of my exposure has been to Northerly versions: *Chucking it down, throwing it down, pissing it down, spitting.* This often gets shortened to simply "chuckin' it." ("Chuckin'" is pronounced *chookin*, like *shook* or *book*.) *Stair-rods* is another descriptor. I don't think I've met a stair-rod in my life, but that doesn't stop me from imagining one: I picture tubular metal weights like those inside the hems of floor-length curtains, except the tubular weights are hammering vertically from the sky: an apt image for the rain's shape and striking force.

Filthy is yet another British designation for unpleasant weather, the word's sonic impact containing all the helpless disgust and fury of the utterer.

I dwell on weather because it offers one of two golden keys (the other is class) to Englishness—its formation; duration, varieties; the modes of response it evokes. Exhibit A: alongside a palette of synonyms for horrible, no-good, very bad weather, the English also maintain an amazingly fertile vocabulary for attitudes of *hopeful-ness* about weather. This is special, elaborately fogged hopefulness, a manifestation—putting it bluntly—of the power of English repression and denial, qualities refined there like no other. That cautious hopefulness remains a national reflex, applying not only to weather but to any obstacle or difficulty—probably rooted in wartime, going back as far as you like. They pride themselves on quietly cultivating a kind of grim (to their minds, stalwart) optimism, generated by the watery idea (no pun) that their shitstorm climate (or war, or brick-stupid politician, or class brutality, or the whole country's ubiquitous, storied alcoholism) might eventually get better. Monty Python satirized this spot-of-bother penchant in a skit featuring John Cleese as a British general whose leg has been bitten off by a tiger, *tut-tutting*, looking off to the distance, drink in hand: "It's nothing; only a leg; damned nuisance, really."

The late author Anita Brookner, among myriad others, sent up this syndrome. One of her novels was actually titled *Making Things Better.* The Brits seem to believe—in a poignant, childlike way, as if wishing the ailing Tinkerbell back into good health—that if you only hope earnestly enough, bear down hard enough—be pure enough of character, strong enough of heart, patient and stoic enough or simply ignore reality airily, insouciantly enough—the hideous weather, the social or economic dragon, the ghastly restaurant/cafe/shop service, the obnoxious, menacing yob, the punishing relationship, will somehow correct itself or slink away.

Also—this can't be overstressed—they consider it bad form to howl, to make a scene.

6.

Form is everything. See the above, tiger-eating-leg response.

Mustn't grumble is a familiar, comforting, Northern-based refrain. In fact it's almost a Northern *raison d'être*, a mission and policy statement. But it also soaks into the larger culture—driven by a notion of what is seemly. (Even though we see footage of the gentlemen and -women of Parliament barking insults at one another during sessions.) The ruling ethos among the general population is one of stoical endurance. Nobody got over the wars, in the sense of psychological recovery, even those born many decades later. Everybody is therefore expected to buck up, like a Royal Air Force (RAF) pilot. Hence the famous *carry on* slogan. One of two behaviors is approved: *Right then; off I'll fly to my almost-certain doom, let's just have one last sip of that cracking good G&T, shall we.*

The other insider motif: *We got through it, didn't we luv.* Getting through, getting by, muddling through, keeping on: the words could serve as a national creed or covenant, and indeed stand to this hour as the preferred measure of anyone's merit. They may never get *over* anything, but they got *through* it. Mettle (quiet, unshowy) signifies far more than achievement. In fact achievement is regarded with complex resistance, with mixed suspicion and resentment. Achievement implies ambition, naked striving, self-aggrandizement, showy competitiveness. These are traits that fill Brits with distaste. Though they may treat the transgressor with exquisite politeness (translation: contempt), they'll already have dismissed that unfortunate perp from serious esteem. They even have a term (Australian in origin) for the offender: the Tall Poppy, meaning a flower that sticks out above the rest (begging, of course, to be whacked back to the heights of the others). Audacity and temerity *per se* are not automatically admired nor rewarded.

This is baffling to Americans, who adore rags-to-riches stories, outlandish heroism, the more lurid the better; soapy-sobby arcs leading to sequins-and-tiaras-triumph. We love to serially revere athletes, talent contestants, reality television heroes (until they get caught out at some debauchery, and then we call for their decapitation and step over their corpses on the way to worship the next new star). In England, though reality television now has a fierce grip, from talent shows to baking shows, with families of contenders weeping in the wings: beneath it all somehow, aspiring *past your place*—your proper (original) class, niche, station—still tends to be viewed as unseemly as public farting. Ambition puzzles and vexes them, including friends and family—maybe friends and family most of all. (Despite its superb education system and the crown-jewel erudition of an Oxbridge history, smart people in England are dismissed by most working-class folk as *right brainboxes*.)

Bearing all this in mind, we return to weather.

It's coomin' braahter now . . . ("It's coming brighter now.") Uttered in broad, Northern vowels, while peering out the window or squinting at the sky. Observed timidly, often by old ladies rushing through vicious lashings of ice-needle rain from bus-stop shelter to bus, or the reverse. The phrase rang so infuriatingly in my ears I started wanting to punch the utterer in the face, timid old lady or not. (And I'm a Unitarian-reared vegan who carries bugs out of the house rather than hurt them.) Those cringing words— their hesitant, mealy hand-wringing—quickly ring almost masochistic to an outsider, as if one were watching people quietly bending over to be thrashed with a paddle (with holes in it) for the past several thousand years. England is an *island in the North Sea*, folks. Why, exactly, might weather suddenly choose to behave as if this were not the case? Those words—*coomin' braahter*—tend to be spoken just before the next blow: the next monsoon-gale, the Brexit vote—the next film or stage play in which the Northerner, inevitably and sadly, is yet again depicted as a stooge.

You want to yell at them. You want to protect them.

Let me pause to remind you, gentle reader: I'm more ashamed and embarrassed of Americans than of anybody else on this earth. Anyone from elsewhere may trash us with perfect accuracy. This is not a contest for whose country may out-stupid or out-blunder the other's—at least not precisely; not here.

Therefore, the most common English posture and facial expression? Hunched, folded, bundled, capped, scarved. Grimacing, huddled. Arms folded tight or hugging the body, slapping its sides or pulling the coat or scarf or collar tighter, smashing the hat to the head to keep it from being whipped off; leaning into the onslaught, fighting to re-right the inside-out umbrella. It's a posture of

Warding Off, Flinching From, Pressing Against at desperate angles—like Chaplin mimes of moving against powerful wind.

What space exists in such a scenario, I ask you, for a relaxed mind?

(Recall the little girl now, dreaming of the future on her warm, Arizona front porch.)

How can calm thought have room to open and air its wings? How can largess of spirit and vision find easeful surroundings? What shelter occurs here for charitable, sympathetic reasoning? For opening one's arms?

It doesn't, and they don't. Open their arms, that is. They keep them folded tight. They stiffen and shrink back if you move in for a hug. They're not huggy or kissy as a rule, unless they're drunk. Sometimes not even then.

Honestly? Weather alone there makes you want to drink. Which, oh man. Do they ever.

7.

Maybe the best way to conclude is to name some good things.

A wise, wry friend once remarked of the French, "They do many things very well." That truth may also be applied to the English—if within, say, a more curtailed scope.

I mean, the country is pretty small.

The English honor arts and letters in ways that put the United States to shame. London—a sovereign planet, remember—presents a true and constant embarrassment of riches. The Tate, the Tate Modern, the National Gallery, the Royal Academy, the Courtauld: these and others stand as Mt. Rushmores of gorgeous adventuresomeness in art, some free, most very affordable, and as such a reprimand to the comparative paltriness of American collections (and prices of access to them). Add in the entire, world-renowned theater district (a bright, bristling scene) and any number of smaller venues showcasing art in multiple forms, bravely and creatively. In the ersatz provinces one finds theaters, galleries, concert halls, and sometimes whole estates repurposed into art centers (sculptor Barbara Hepworth's, for one). And even in small industrial towns you'll spot community theaters, music halls, and serious film centers where people push their pay-what-you-can donation into a slotted jar before settling back for an evening of "Cinema Paradiso."

Let us praise the British Museum; its beautiful Library. Likewise London's bookstores; famous, brilliantly stocked, gloriously independent: Charing Cross. Bloomsbury. *The London Review of Books* bookstore. Also the hole-in-the-wall, cobwebby-creaky, aged-treasures bookstores. All these lay out a serious, revolving feast, enough to make any bibliophile or student or artist start to whimper with happiness. An unspoken, almost worshipful understanding permeates the atmospheres of these refuges. Browsers are left in peace until or unless they ask for help. Staff are knowledgeable. You want to kiss them, but—*hmmph.* A quiet *thanks very much* does fine.

One can only implore our own gatekeepers: Look well.

Somehow alongside the working-class English distrust of intelligentsia, the general population overall is full-tilt crazy for certain cultural practices and bodies of knowledge. One is what my husband calls parlor games: hangman, charades, Pictionary. They love old rock and roll; pride themselves on knowing every word of every song since Chuck Berry, Bill Haley, and Fats Domino. They adore pub quizzes (trivia quizzes), even in the most zipped-up, sullen little outbacks; people go to pains to attend them, often driving some distance through crappy weather. These sessions can go for hours, stipulating elaborate subject realms and rules (no smartphones allowed, though how they enforce this is beyond me, and I suspect that many a "winner" bent that rule). They also savor a sprightly bouquet of television quiz shows along the lines of what's my line, truth-or-lies, or college bowl formats, as well as late-night talk shows run by bewilderingly clever hosts like Graham Norton, Rob Brydon, and Stephen Fry. (Fry seems to be everywhere simultaneously; one assumes there's a Stephen Fry channel showing on

English telly day and night, even while one glimpses him in person at the posh department store Fortnum & Mason—and good grief that gentleman is *big*, a kind of friendly giant.) The quiz shows tend to pit celebrities or ultragifted students against one another answering whimsically imagined questions, and it's humbling to watch the wit and scholarship fly, like multicolored pendants dancing in the wind. (A surprising number of working-class households pay careful attention to these near-incomprehensible recitals of mathematical, linguistic, and scientific formulae. Maybe they hope some of the knowledge may rub off or osmose, by proximity.) The late-night talk shows let bad language and anecdotes of doubtful taste bubble over as they please. You get to see sides of American celebrities, when they appear as guests there, that you'd never see or hear in the US. Strikingly—given the national ethos of repression and straitlaced containment—the atmosphere on British airwaves is much freer, raunchier, funnier, more fun, than we might remotely dream of seeing at home. A novice viewer feels, tuning in, as though she's stumbled into a cocktail party. It probably is.

The Stately Homes business (I'm struck by that demure title) is always touching, and impressive. The Brits have found ways to restore once-wealthy, left-to-crumble estates into handsome, burnished venues for public enjoyment: typically some rambling, ornate manor or mansion with appurtenances—stables, walking paths, lush private parks and gardens—often set in fairy-tale countryside, rich green hills in all directions. The caretakers charge a modest admission, and strolling tourists always include plenty of Brits, snapping photos like maniacs. The houses (sometimes castles) are often imposing, elaborate, and aged in ways Americans simply cannot understand (until they've wandered a good long time in the UK and Europe, where bits of Greek and Roman ruins casually, continually surface). What these lordly piles convey straightaway is a sense of how a privileged slice of the population was able to live during a particular period (some in *Downton Abbey* fashion). These places can be drafty and musty, which only confirms their dignified authenticity. They smell old. Sometimes they contain secret passages, attics, hidden cupboards, and dungeons; even moats with drawbridges. Sometimes they contain terrific art—or terrifically bad art. Often they are filled with beautiful, rare antique furniture, carpets, kitchen tools and pantry fittings, swords, armor, historic utensils and appurtenances. Outdoors one might find sculptures, or topiary still maintained in whimsical shapes—sometimes an actual maze. Often a handful of guides and docents stand patiently at strategic points to answer questions or brightly offer almanac-like information, even if you didn't ask, or gently warn you away from things you're not supposed to touch or step on. They tend to be elderly, somewhat frail, eagerly sincere. One's heart cracks a bit to imagine how little—if anything—the kind older gentleman or gentlewoman may be paid for this homespun touch. The Brits (at least a certain demographic of them) are quite big on volunteerism.

May I add here: they relish the word *quite*. Americans recognize the Britishism as a one-word confirmation, as "indeed" or "very much so." But Brits also love to say *I quite like*—naming whatever the liked thing is. The structure of this declaration has always struck me as piquant, a sprightly archaism, refined and, I'm sorry to point out, completely irrelevant. (I hasten to add: Americans too love announcing their tastes, and in the end nobody cares about what we quite like, either.) In any case, the docents and guides of Stately Homes seem to love what they do. And haven't we learned that that is pretty much as good as it gets?

As to food, first, the caveats: I'm neither a foodie nor a junk-eater. (I quite like fresh fruit and vegetables.) Judgment here deserves to remain flexible—relative to what may be available in the hour of need, and also dependent upon the judge's relationship to food in general. Is the judge a fine-dining gourmand? That won't be useful, unless that person has piles of extra money. Is the judge equable and open to different ways and tastes? That will serve better.

Weather, unsurprisingly, enforces traditions and tastes in

English food, going back to days of coach inns (and further, if you will, to pots of whatever was stewing in cauldrons over chimney fires). If it's cold, wet, and freezing outside—which of course it is—you're not likely to crave a salad. (I myself may crave a salad, but I would not be usual.) Most normal humans will want to get as many calories into themselves as fast as they possibly can, washed back with heavy wines and ales and whiskeys and any other *neck oil* you can *get down your gob* (bona fide terminology).

So one still finds the proud, sturdy traditions: roasts, chops, and game, many with rich sauces or (they adore this) *en croute* as pasties, or meat or fish pies (including, yes, steak and kidney). Potatoes persist in every form, especially chips (fries). Other vegetables may be an afterthought, too often an overcooked one. But the phenomenon called mushy peas (and pub grub in general) remains a triumph: warming, flavorful. A quiet point of pride is British cheese, in artisanal forms and flavors. Actually, much British food tends to taste damn good. How good some of it may be *for* you—another discussion. But the Brits are actually laboring with dedicated hearts (and eyes on economic indicators) to create high-end, delicious, healthy food, often thematic, trying to incorporate modern versions of an old dish like, say, shepherd's pie. This can seem, sometimes, a little fantastic. Beets in fancy forms are still beets, as are winter vegetables. At least there's hope now they won't be boiled to death, the time-honored way.

The Brits revere what's called a classic English breakfast, meaning sausage (yes, they love blood sausage) and/or bacon, eggs, a slice or two of tomato, beans (like Americans' pork and beans) ladled onto toast, dosed with a sauce that's close to what we know to be Worcestershire. They dive into these as if it were their last meal on earth. It all seems a little gross in one way, attractive in another, depending how you've been raised and how you feel about these foodstuffs in general. I'll take a salad, thanks. And they do, thank God, offer lots of lovely salads. They also do fish well, including fish and chips, and if they serve it wrapped in newsprint these days, that's a kind of holdover affectation.

They love sweets and bakeries. They have a trillion cafes.

And tea is constant. So constant it drives one batty. Does it really help them live longer or think better? Who knows. I must describe a crisp afternoon of playing various sports and games outdoors with relatives and friends (may they never read this, and if they do, may they not plan to shoot me) in a big, pretty, green field. When the assembled company stamped indoors (and it was chilly outside but it was *late afternoon*), what did the hosts offer their guests? A trayful of cups of *lukewarm tea with milk in it*. I was aghast, dying for a cold beer. When I gathered courage to ask for one, they directed me primly to a couple of mild-mannered Heinekens kept at room temperature.

These are the trials.

They're hugely proud of their National Health System (NHS), which, to an outsider, seems to work reasonably well—certainly nearly anything is better than the ruins of a health-care system the United States now flounders with. I have seen, though, that the English must often wait long periods of time for surgeries. Maybe if that's the worst that can be said about the NHS, it's no sin. I've not looked more closely, because I don't want to. I could interview friends and family, but I think they'd seize the opportunity to complain, which is their right, but not here.

Likewise, I can't discuss British politics because I have never understood it (despite my husband's patient lectures and occasional rants), except to know it's class-ruled and often bitterly unjust. What else, I'd ask, may be new in politics? Better for me to stand away. I confess, though, to a certain generic shame for Tony Blair, for his having sold out to George W. Bush. Note how Blair has since effectively vanished, that last so-called bold gesture making toast of him. In the words of Alexander Hamilton's amused buddies (in the fabulous hip-hop musical) when they discover Hamilton's checkbook stubs for payments to silence a married lover: "He not goin' be President now."

(Except in America nowadays, that level of foolery wouldn't count as couch change.)

It's so sadly clear that—paraphrasing the braggy song from *Annie Get Your Gun*—any stupidity or atrocity or ham-handed wrong the Brits can commit, we Americans can out-commit. I'm hardly proud of this. And in the end I offer the Brits a hearty handshake (a hug if they're willing). That sceptered isle still, in the main, provides a green and pleasant land; just keep your rain gear handy. Their systems, in the broad view, still mostly work— sometimes shamingly better than ours. Exempting the petty exas- perations, foolish bigotry, and obvious crimes? They're a good bunch. They like to laugh, eat, drink, obsess over beloved soccer and *Dancing with the Stars*. They're not a rapacious lot, at least in latter incarnations. They're our cousins, overall better read and hands-down better mannered, and, at heart, extremely decent. We need to play nicely. We go back.

Location Sluts

"The author divides her time between . . ."

Paris and Santa Barbara. San Francisco and Tuscany.

Portland, Maine, and Kealakekua, Hawaii. The New Hampshire woods and Manhattan.

Yeah, yeah. Los Angeles and Tahiti. Positano and Cape Cod. Bozeman and Tokyo.

God, how I hate these declarations, often the final flourish in an About the Author bio, generally found on the backs of book jackets or at the ends of articles. I mean no disrespect, but—really. Don't you at least briefly hate these, too? Or at least raise an eyebrow?

Quickly: what's your first thought, viewing such claims?

Mine snaps down like a mousetrap:

Well, how delightful. It only falls to the rest of us wretched peasants—we who've just one home—to envision the author relishing this stately division.

Of course, certain presumptions are built in: lucky-devil author has earned or inherited or married or partnered a financial instrument sufficient to arrange Living The Dream. (Occasionally: Author lives and works in Y, partner lives and works in X; the couple migrates back and forth.) More subtly, such biographical glitter suggests that the author has carefully chosen what they hold to be the two best-possible places on earth—and the best times of year for living in each of them.

Are you, reader, presently nested in either of those places? No? Ah, too bad for you, then.

End of story.

Except, not. The casual report of two homes in two locations sets rolling, in a reader's mind, a little caravan of unwanted thoughts that begin wandering off in different directions like a loosed herd of confused moose. First thoughts might be envious: *Gee, I wish I could live that way, too.* Other thoughts might mosey into a dark forest of dismay, in which the reader accuses herself of not having done so well—not paid the right kind of attention, not acted prudently or shrewdly enough, failed to sell film rights— whatever it would have taken to afford setting up and squatting in two homes in two fabulous locales.

A friend once insisted that when you return from an extended trip, you have about ten minutes to clearly see your own surroundings for what they are. Generally, the impression makes you wince: endearing, but funky. Slightly shabby, if lovable. Those back-door stairs—splintery. That front porch plank, sagging deeper. When did the paint wear off the wainscoting? How did the windows get so dirty; the screens so nasty? And yikes, those smudge marks.

Jacket-flap declarations ("divides her time between . . . ") have a way of waking our personal ten minutes of clarity with a small crack of lightning—kind of like the Bride of Frankenstein—every time we read them.

Maybe most authors don't give a damn about what gongs are struck in a reader's head when they view these graceful claims. Possibly the authors hardly think about it, or assume the material gets ignored. Maybe they didn't write it themselves; maybe their publicists did.

Interestingly, I've known people with two homes. Sometimes one home is seasonal: a summer retreat, untenable in winter. Either way, to me the reality of owning two places sounds . . . unsettled. How, I've wondered, could you really feel situated—as the British say, *sorted*—if you must have two of everything, keep two of everything in good repair, and, relatedly, realized too often that your favorite version of the desired thing (clothing, shoes, tools, pills, sporting goods, kitchen paraphernalia) is stowed at the other place? (The *other place* will inevitably acquire a name, shorthand for easy reference: "The Cabin," "The Apartment," "New York," "Shangri-La.") I've also wondered about the cost and effort of maintaining two venues: houseplants, pets, bills, mail, routine domestic chores. I think as well of the strange, human, greener-grass syndrome: feeling pulled toward the other property, no matter where you may presently be camped. (Is it Tolstoy or Chekhov who depicts a character longing for the dacha once installed in the city, then immediately craving the pied-à-terre after removing himself to the country?)

Does the above qualify as sour grapes? As a way of telling ourselves, "since we can't afford such luxury, let's find reasons to decide that it's a not-necessarily-desirable way to live"?

I can neither confirm nor deny.

Let me distract you at this point with a game my husband and I never tire of playing. It often starts while we're in motion, staring at other locales; walking, driving, in a plane, or on a train.

If we could afford it, the game always begins—quickly appended by, "if Joan were able to sell film rights to one of her novels," followed by Joan swallowing hard—*which place would we like to live in, part of the year?* Where would we just flat-out buy a house or cottage or apartment, because we are pretending we absolutely could?

This is a hella delicious game. Convenient. Gratifying. It costs nothing. It risks nothing—nobody else knows we're doing it; therefore we court no judgment, no contrarianism, no scorn. Best, it's wide open as the sky. All options are feasible; money is no object. And for a festive bonus—since husband and self have internalized each other's habits and natures—a preestablished hierarchy of biases and prejudices automatically clicks into position. We're in heated agreement.

Assumption one: No wintering. We don't do cold.

Assumption two: Blue and green. That's code for natural beauty. Only word-class cities (London, Paris, Rome, New York) may be semi-exempt from the blue-and-green criterion. And even they, thank God, through handsome parks and appending countryside, may offer precious slices of it.

Assumption three: Humane, arts-loving, simpatico vibes. Diversity across ages, ethnicities, demographics. A dash of whimsy, of playfulness, wouldn't hurt. (France is good at that, believe it or not.)

The rest of our preferences are easy to predict. Vibrant culture, physical ease, access to healthy food. No sense listing various talismanic places here—everyone has their own such list. Then, depending how exercised we've become, we go through our list of contenders, venue by venue, and unpack each one—and ultimately (wait for it) decide why each choice is perhaps finally *not quite* the bulls-eye choice: why in fact it's probably better (freer, cheaper, easier) just to rent some space in that place whenever we feel like it, rather than buy outright. Soon we pretty much forget about even renting there, and we feel better yet. Think of all the money and heartache we've just saved! Realtor's fees! Gasoline! Guilt for not being wherever we aren't!

Then we resume the lives we're leading—a little lighter around the heart, sighing with refreshed clarity—noticing too, with quicker pleasure as we go about our days, the abundance of particulars that make us happy about where we actually live.

As I say, all this costs nothing, except some thinking and talking. And the reward is real: renewed gratitude and appreciation for our present humble setup.

Here's a cousin game to the above. Though it involves gusts of imagination, it feels effortless while in progress. As reliably as a tapped knee causes a shin to kick, whenever we visit an attractive city or town we immediately begin to think, in the course of exploring it, *Hey, We Could Live Here.*

It's the damnedest phenomenon.

We begin to stare with great urgency at the layouts of neighborhoods, conditions of houses, downtowns, landscapes fore and aft. We start counting up cafes, libraries, theaters, parks, schools, ethnic eateries; qualities of public transport, ratios of trees to streets.

We search people's faces (for expressions of contentment); we size up their general bearing and bien-être. We have gone so far as to drop in at the local Chamber of Commerce to collect a packet of informational flyers intended for new residents, usually titled Welcome To Our City.

Weather figures, naturally. All the elements named on the pre-established hierarchy, figure. In our minds, rapidly, we set up a Typical Day in the New Location. We picture ourselves beginning that day holding a cup of excellent coffee, likely standing at a big, clean window, gazing out to the lovely lawns and fir trees (or the orange and lemon trees, or papaya and banana, or the desert cacti, or the exciting, hipster-urban center several stories below us) that we've so long admired. In no time our eyes start to shine, our voices to quicken, as each item on our list of necessities seems to be checked. *We could ride our bikes from home to the library, and to coffee. Terrific coffee! Bookstores! Food trucks! We could subscribe to the Little Theater. Take or teach classes. I'm sure there's a gym here somewhere. How pleasant these streets, this park, this art museum!*

And then—at first slowly, then rather fast—we forget about it.

Other tasks tug at our attention. If the adored city is part of a tour, we carry on visiting different cities and towns, where similar, whirlwind romances flare up. Like children freshly fixated on a new toy, we swiftly shed the last fixation: the town or city where, mere days or weeks ago, we'd meticulously begun to plot spending the rest of our lives. We seldom look back.

What confounds me is how easily this happens; how lightly we float away from what began as something close to passion. My guess? That it's the intangibles, the unseen furnishings and assets of our present setting, which make themselves felt and call us back—with very little conscious awareness on our parts. Those intangibles include a deeply entrenched network (small but sturdy) of friends. None of them is Einstein, but most are thoughtful and kind. Most have known us so long that the simple fact of their nearby presence—the embedded understanding of their automatic, earnest support—seems at this point to help flesh out our own comprehension of ourselves. Were we to yank up stakes and drop them elsewhere, it could take, we sense, quite a long time to meet and make new friends—to move past the pleasant-novelty-of-contact phase into a state of genuine friendship. At our ages, that chunk of time signifies. Other familiarities fan out for review: patterns of movement. Proximity to other cities where we have family, other longtime friends, and other pleasurable patterns. All these considerations urge us, paraphrasing Fagin's immortal words, to "think we'd better think it out again."

It might not, after all, be the most enviable state—touching down by turns in two communities, without meaningfully belonging to either.

Perhaps, of course, that's not always the case.

And yet.

This game, by the way, is called *Location Sluts*.

Might it look impressive, do you think, in a biographical statement?

The Room Where It Happens

Think of the word *hotel*.

Run the sound of it through the mind's ear.

Something internal quickens. The sound stirs something beyond explaining, something that feels at once ancient and modern.

Give the word room to sink and ripple out, tapping at nerve receptors. Feel its history in your body; feel the two-syllable utterance snap open the little treasure chest packed behind your heart. *Pop*, the spring-lid flips back; out waft the ghosts, fairies, demons—gossamer and wispy, hard and burnished, sweaty and fleshy.

Let's go to a hotel. Let's get a hotel.

My hotel. Our hotel. Your hotel.

Hotel.com!

It's a thing. Oh, is it ever.

Let the free-associating begin.

Crisp sheets smelling faintly of bleach—or fuzzed and nubby with wear. Pillowcases bearing track marks—faint, repeated black arcs you first think must be traces of mascara but realize, after long puzzling, are imprints from black sleep masks.

Sparkling (or smudged) water glasses. Cunning minibar bottles. Laminated menus for expensive food, or a flyer from the local pizzeria. Carpet pleasantly spongy under bare feet—or carpet that has given up, stained and matted, trampled evidence of uncountable years.

Drapes the colors of a showroom window—or a faded polaroid.

White noise of nearby freeway traffic; a semi's plaintive,

receding horn. Or the muffled honks and clamor of a downtown avenue, many floors below.

A vast bed piled with useless decorative pillows. Or a saggy cot. Bathrooms big enough to hold a party in—or a curtained-off space the size of a phone booth. Black marble countertops—or black mold blooming on decrepit tiles. Scent of Occitane or gin, cleaning fluid or mildew. Somber prints on the wall: rainy, late-afternoon street scenes with blurry shop windows and car headlights prowling the gloom.

A thick, convex peephole in the door, wizened as an elephant's eye; its unspoken caveat: *beware whomever's out there.*

Other poignant ideas of safety and surety scatter among these memories like anthropological tokens: the tarnished gold chain that slides across the separation between door and wall, believed (touchingly) to stop any foe. Deadbolts that click into place above the lock cylinder, trusting that an extra stick of metal, small as a candy bar, will seal out a threatening world.

For that is the hotel's irreducible pledge: fortressing. Safekeeping. The world, its weather, its creatures—held off, walled out, at least for the night.

At the heart of that pledge dwells the space to which we entrust our bodies and belongings, where we rest and replenish: the *room*, *chambre*, *salle*, *camera*, *zimmer*, *habitación*, the compartment bounded by walls and ceiling in which we place ourselves, our clothing, money, documents, toiletries—where we bathe, have sex, eat and drink and sleep, watch terrible television, or (rarer and rarer) read. A room's appointments, be they lavish or bare-bones—a rocking chair, a balcony, a penal cell's lidless toilet and bunk— these particulars vibrate, to the sensitive viewer, with emotional power. The simplest object—that brave yellow chair in Van Gogh's room at Arles—tells the story of our functions and needs, wrought like sap from human experience across centuries. These are the tools we've agreed we require in order to repair, restore. Their quality runs a wide range, crude to decadent. Towel racks, a mirror, a miniature refrigerator—a lumpy pallet, a nail in a wall.

What's more difficult to accept—to describe—is any room's blank neutrality, its obdurate thingness, its technical nullity. Void of thought or judgment, the structure that contains us (into which we are born, and in some form of which most of us will likely end) is first and last inert matter, not caring what form it takes or what happens within or outside it, whether we deface it or burn it down. It maintains a uniform, bland impartiality.

Does the placement of a Bible in the nightstand drawer suggest our culture's nervous sense of what may, by some pernicious reflex, be on a traveler's mind? Might the presence of the book mean to dissuade us, or—failing that—stand in for last rites?

I think of a scene from the film *The Front* about the years of communist witch-hunts and blacklisting of artists in Hollywood. One of the writers so evilly targeted, played by Zero Mostel, enters an upper-story, swanky hotel room he has just engaged. He nods placidly as the porter shows him around. Wearing a porkpie hat shoved back on his greasy head—looking like a children's television show host gone to seed—he tips the porter; tips the wine steward who's wheeled in a cloth-covered table bearing a bottle in a silver ice bucket. Mostel smiles an impossibly sad smile; hums, mutters. When the waitstaff has left he takes a swig straight from the bottle and, still smiling and humming, carries it offscreen cradled in one arm. We hear a sudden, horribly unidentifiable sound, and in a second the camera cuts to the open window's blowing curtains.

That, too, is a hotel.

Wikipedia tells us a few things: ". . . derived from the French hôtel (hostel, from Latin *hospes, hospitis*, a stranger, foreigner, thus a guest) . . . a building seeing frequent visitors, and providing care . . . "

And:

Facilities offering hospitality to travelers have been a feature of the earliest civilizations. In Greco-Roman culture and ancient Persia, hospitals for recuperation and rest were built at thermal baths. Japan's Nishiyama Onsen Keiunkan, founded in 705, was officially recognised by the Guinness World Records as the oldest hotel in the world. During the Middle Ages, various religious orders at monasteries and abbeys would offer accommodation for travellers on the road. . . .

The precursor to the modern hotel was the inn of medieval Europe, possibly dating back to the rule of Ancient Rome. These would provide for the needs of travelers, including food and lodging, stabling and fodder for the traveler's horse(s) and fresh horses for the mail coach.

Frequent visitors. Foreigners or strangers who became guests. Provision of care—later, of accommodation. Food and drink, a bed, and when apt, stabling, fodder, fresh horses.

These simple descriptions move me sharply, in much the way my husband feels moved by museum displays of ancient glassware, dishes, and utensils. However technologically proficient we may now be, however streamlined our present era, he marvels, "there seem to be only so many ways you can drink from a cup and eat from a plate." To those functions I suppose we may add: only so many ways one could sleep, love, laugh, cry, fear, desire, suffer, feel conflicted or inspired, remorseful or lonely—then or now. I think he liked that linking of images, of gestures and needs, across millennia. It soothes and startles. *They were like us.*

A similar, groggy recognition riffles through us when we see, for instance, a preserved, ancient sandal or boot. In its sole we can make out a human foot's shape or imprint. The same feeling infuses us, when you think about it, to see the preserved foot itself.

Since I can remember owning speech, the word *hotel* has called up excitement; dizzying, intoxicating. My mother, bored and lonely during endless, baking Phoenix days while my handsome father was away teaching, lecturing, appearing on television panels—and other investigations we little girls could not imagine but that she sadly, correctly sensed—would drive my sister and me in our dust-covered, olive-drab '49 Ford to the Westward Ho Hotel or Ramada Inn or Desert Inn (glam destinations then) or to similar, cheerful westerly resorts. These establishments pitched themselves as family friendly; to us they embodied magic. (To this hour I don't know how our mother—painfully shy—arranged our use of the pools without our being guests there. Maybe she paid a nominal fee, or perhaps in those days they occasionally allowed it for public relations' sake.) The word *hotel* squeezed our already-fast-pumping hearts, promising a rainbow of pleasures; these danced before our imaginations in multisensory detail: a bright-turquoise, chlorine-scented pool, its mysterious deep end painted a thrillingly darker turquoise—in which we spent so many hours our fingertips and tiptoes wrinkled up like prunes. *Hotel* meant ice— for *free*—from machines that kept noisily cranking out mountains more. It meant smells of Coppertone, cigarettes, coffee, frying burgers. It meant grown-ups in sunglasses seated poolside on chaises longues sipping nose-tickling alcoholic drinks and chatting in tones of ironic collusion while keeping a tired eye on their kids. Andrie and I, inexhaustible, made up water games: competitions to touch the bottom, cannonballs and somersaults, diving for any trinket that would sink to the pool's floor, standing on our hands, floating on our backs. We sang to each other underwater, taking turns guessing (after bursting to the surface panting) what the song had been. "Jingle Bells" was a favorite.

Now, as an older woman with a lifetime's trove of images (pensions, motels, dorm rooms, bed-and-breakfasts, campsites, skyscraper suites) in store, the thrall of the word hotel expands to include every aspect customarily listed as an amenity: candy and soda machines, hot tubs and pools, furniture (or its lack), bars or restaurants (or their lacks), deportment of staff and guests alike—and always, from young adulthood at least, the sub-rosa implication of sex, imagined or real. What hotels ignite in our (now adult) memories is the long rearview, jumbled and compacted: what Louise Erdrich called "that closet stuffed with savage mementos," surfaces and textures, smells and sounds, temperatures, personalities, voices. Above all, what hotels promise to reveal—despite their official privacy and sanctuary—are secrets. A physical facility guards its own history, wittingly or not, behind facades, in crannies, alleyways, chambers, cubbies, corridors. So do the people it holds. We move closer when we can, to catch a glimpse, to eavesdrop. Salacious or sad, shocking or silly, news creeps forth (or drops on our heads) after first impressions prove incomplete, thin, or plain false. Who's falling in or out of love. Who's sneaking around. Who's addicted. Who's benumbed, enraged, disgusted, euphoric, enflamed with longing or entombed in despair.

Who's preening. Who's hiding.

(What lamps are broken. What the remote gets and does not get.)

Three memories:

One. My husband (traveling with a male friend) slipped onto a barstool in Bali one evening, and in a moment noticed an owl seated calmly on the stool next to him. He does not remember what the owl may have been drinking.

Two. We checked into a hotel in Bordeaux, France, on a chilly day in early spring; I turned around from the reception counter to idly gaze at the lobby and caught sight of a very old, frail man slowly ascending the lobby's curved staircase, smiling—despite his frailty, and the effort of climbing the stairs—with undisguised, anticipatory delight. Behind him, patiently pacing her own ascent to his, was a young woman of mixed race who also bore a pleased smile.

Three. Being wakened at dawn in a Best Western perched on a low cliff near the Oregon coast—by a swarm of bikers firing up, in unison, their dozen or more Harleys to take off on that day's "run," which in biker-ese means mass migration. The sound was something like an erupting volcano coinciding with an earthquake.

Really? I thought as the room shook and roared, glass rattling in the panes. *Really?*

This seething kaleidoscope, to a writer, transmutes into the rich loam of art: films, plays, novels, stories. A hotel supplies the

near-ideal setting for storytelling because it is a cutaway of community, self-contained, a true hive, everyone handily approxi-
mate to everyone else. Basic needs being met, what comes next?
Who wanders out to make trouble or attract it? Who begins to
divulge true colors? Who goes to great pains to camouflage them?
Of course setting itself becomes a character: component and
enabler, the auspice overarching all antics like a raised theater
curtain, promising revelations; absorbing movement, sheltering
strangeness and eccentricity.

The perfect microcosm. The perfect stage—hiding its own falli-
bilities and oddnesses.

Any building carries its own story. Look up at your ceiling:
what happened there? Who remodeled? When did they paint
over that old light fixture and install a smoke alarm? Who did
the work? Were they paid decently? Were they good to their families? Are they still alive? What do they regret; what are they
proud of? Was that faint rectangular indentation a trap door?
Look under the bed. Look where surfaces join; the faded patches
in the wallpaper. Look at the caulked-over places near the
plumbing fixtures, the outlines of what once was—in some
prior, more luxe, en suite arrangement—an adjoining door.
Sometimes you can read part of a building's story in small visual
cues, architectural flourishes or lapses—like the cross section of
a tree trunk's rings—to begin to discern what a poet friend calls
"the seams in the seamlessness."

This may also lead to a phenomenon of place that fascinates and
horrifies, like a cobra rising and swaying before us.

Picture a hotel in Puerto Vallarta that billed itself as luxury,
exclusive, all-containing (standard lures for frightened Americans
like me, who wanted to feel protected and served and safe inside
its walls).

We brought our then-twelve-year-old (my stepson, now a
kind, wry, worldly young man). The hotel was perched on a portion of (not clean or pretty) beach, its formal grounds cordoned
off by lengths of rope laid on the sand, with guards patrolling

those cordons. Ragged vendors of junk stood sadly on the other side of the defining rope—a sad, embattling experience for the unwary guest wandering out. Dotting the hills beyond we could spot a few shanties, a cooking fire burning in front of some of them, several goats. In the air one whiffed the fire's smoke, and a faintest hint of fleshly decay. Yes, the hotel itself seemed at first glance big and luxurious—its low, connected structures painted warm pinks and tangerines; a swim-up bar in the gigantic, heated pool; waitstaff bringing food and drinks to lounging guests (rashly expensive, we soon learned; thereafter avoided). But after a few days of pacing along the corridors from sprawling restaurant to multistory lobby with its jungly, rooftop-tall cage of exotic, screeching birds, back to our slow-ceiling-fan-lulled rooms, the layout began to feel finite, even fake; someone's construct—which of course it was—a thin, porous facade like a film set. The staff, like most hotel staff and service workers everywhere on earth, did its best to be polite. But the strain of meeting managerial standards, of safeguarding jobs they depended upon to support who knew how many others, seemed permanently stenciled onto their faces, and their unconscious expressions' resting position was that of someone enduring intense stomach cramps.

As if to rhyme with that, the boy contracted intestinal humbug from the restaurant's food. Then he developed severe infections in both ears, from a few minutes spent cavorting in the actual ocean.

Guests were encouraged never to leave the premises, nor to bring in food or drink from elsewhere. Unsurprisingly, it was difficult to get into town, or to a store.

It wasn't long before I began to grasp that this luxury retreat, sold as part of a package including airfare, might easily be viewed as a high-end prison, wherein we guests (families, students, couples, retirees) actually served as its clueless inmates, except that we were paying money for this temporary trick of artifice, the trompe l'oeil: we were the trick's noisy, clueless, overfed marks, its fools.

Were reflections like mine corrupt, ungrateful, first-world-contaminated? Was I a snob, condemning those innocents wanting only to give themselves and their spouses and families and friends a no-strings good time? I would argue that mine was simply a human noticing. That this *inversion*, where what first presents as *le ne plus ultra* soon morphs into a rouged-up jail or zoo—is a logical and common syndrome, a predictable second shoe falling, part two of the one-two punch any thoughtful observer sees coming yet volunteers to encounter again and again all over the world. Impressions of effervescence, adventure, glamour, and mystery give way without warning to the unretouched: the limiting walls, repeating faces, gestures, voices, psyches.

Islands, hospitals, ocean liners, trains, attics. *Murder on the Orient Express. Ship of Fools. Lord of the Flies. Magic Mountain. Death in Venice. Room with a View. The Diary of Anne Frank. The Longest Journey.*

Psycho—its terrifying Bates Motel.

I'm not saying that the worst must occur in any contained-ensemble situation. In children's literature that containment is practically a staple, lighting and warming our memories: *Madeline. Eloise.* A boarding school supplies a similar laboratory: *The Prime of Miss Jean Brodie; Goodbye, Mr. Chips; Dead Poets' Society; The Loneliness of the Long-Distance Runner; A Separate Peace.* I'm suggesting that the sequestering of a human group leads sooner or later to what we might call a reconfigured understanding. That movement, from expectation to altered understanding, surely mimics the way we finally come to perceive all of life and living. What tugs at our attention in stories doesn't only reduce to soap operas or rubbernecking, though such impulses remain bound up in them. Collect a group of people in a framed space, wait, and watch. To borrow a title from the work of the brilliant young actor/monologist Dan Hoyle: *Tings, Dey Happen.*

As a writer, a shiver still zings my spine when I spot the word hotel in books or films or songs, old and new. Again and again I marvel at what it shakes loose—more complex and numinous and reverberant than simple Pavlovian associations with swimming-pool chlorine and frying burgers (though those remain part of it).

Hotel du Lac. Hotel de Dream. Hotel New Hampshire. Hotel on the Corner of Bitter and Sweet. I Hotel. The White Hotel. Inn of the Sixth Happiness.

Grand Hotel. Grand Budapest Hotel. Second Best Exotic Marigold Hotel. Hotel Silence (Icelandic Literature Prize). *Up in the Old Hotel. Welcome to the Hotel California.*

Recently, I spotted a new book blurbed on social media, whose illustration struck me at once: a miniature cutaway of tiny rooms in a doll-sized hotel or apartment house. In each room reposed two or three articles—a piano, a sink, a bed, a bathtub, a birdbath, a cradle, an armchair—mini-emblems of the stories unfurling within: a kind of *Rear Window*, multiplied.

Human curiosity proves inexhaustible. What goes on in those rooms?

Imagine a list of all the hotel-titled or hotel-themed art we've ever made. Amor Towles set almost the entirety of his fat novel, *A Gentleman in Moscow*, inside that city's (real) Metropole Hotel. Towles wound up his story at its start, as if with a music-box key, and set it playing by arranging that his warmhearted, aristocratic protagonist be sentenced, as lawful punishment, to live the rest of his life in that hotel. Nearly the whole account—a span of some forty years—takes place inside the Metropole's walls.

I'm proposing that the notion *hotel* administers a small electric shock, briefly stopping the muzziness of daily obsession, clearing the decks for the (welcome) disruption of a new, crisply enclosed story. By enclosed I mean fenced off from the ebb-and-surge mess of life, fixed in space and time, dimensional, sensuous, peopled by a distinct cast; grounded in the palpable, peekaboo, multitasking honeycomb of the edifice where it happens. Think, for a crude analogy, of full-sized mannequins whirring toward each other from the side entrances of clock towers, performing their gestures (dancing, drinking, striking a bell with a mallet) and whirring back whence they came. Think of Punch and Judy bonking each other over the head with nightsticks. A hotel is a stage but also a rabbit hole, even sometimes a Brigadoon. Once guests are installed, look out. Author Rachel Ingalls set one story, "On Ice" (from her masterful collection *I See A Long Journey*) in a fancy Swiss hotel. As her luckless protagonist, who has innocently wandered in, soon learns—a special consequence lies in wait. Guests may never be permitted to leave, because time has stopped inside for those lucky (or unlucky) denizens.

Lights, characters, action! the word *hotel* cries out to us. At the same time, it urges us to stop, wait, listen—the way an ancient, oral salvo cried out to hush an unruly audience: *Now, now to the beginning of time, when there were no stories to tell.* And no matter how strangely things may evolve—we are all in. We watch and wonder. Decks have been cleared. Something's about to transpire. We want to fling ourselves toward the pending mystery, see it unfold, have a part in it.

They're like us.

Lundi Matin

Some mental snapshots from travel stay with you forever, floating forward at odd intervals like stubborn ghosts. Here is one,
years old but vivid.

My husband and I are in Paris at the end of one of his teaching
semesters there. I've taken an anxious leave from my receptionist
day job, fearing they will fire me because of my long absence
though they'd officially agreed to it. (They did indeed fire me.) And
though it is May the weather is typically, grimly Parisian: gray and
damp and drizzly, cold and colorless—grisaille, Saul Bellow called
it. We are hell-bent on fleeing grisaille. We have packed to make
our ways to any warmer place. And because we are generally pretty
broke during the period I'm speaking of, we are lugging our bags
onto the métro (French subway) to get to the train station, since
those are the cheapest options.

It is Monday morning.

"We'll travel on a Monday!" one of us had crowed to the other,
who'd instantly agreed when we'd brainstormed our escape plan.
"That way we'll avoid the weekend crowds!"

Superbe. And our great mission carries us in a wash of excited
momentum to the métro station, where we drag and twist and
trundle our luggage up and down the maze of Escher-like stairs
and nonfunctioning escalators, along windswept, urine-smelling
corridors past the accordionists and violinists and sleeping clo-
chards (bums), until we reach the correct platform and the métro
car's doors crank open to the sound of that heartless, futuristic

electronic *beeep* echoing through the tunnel. We grunt and grimace and hoist our bags aboard. And only after the doors have slammed shut, serenaded by another pitiless *beeep*, do we look up from our herded duffels and satchels to find ourselves standing at the front of a packed car of commuters.

The car is silent.

Every seat is filled, so we have no choice but to remain standing before them like mendicants or entertainers, gazing out on the sea of faces positioned toward us. Except those faces are not seeing us. Each face, around age thirty, is pale as death, empty-eyed, blueish half circles beneath. The fluorescent light in the car adds to their pallor. Each face stares straight ahead into nothing. As the car rocks and sways, all heads and shoulders rock and sway with it like clothes bobbing from a line, as if the owners of those heads and shoulders had relinquished volition—their faces void, numb, miserable.

A transport of ghosts.

They are traveling to their jobs, jobs they need to continue to live. From the looks of it, they also bitterly hate those jobs. And they've all (from the looks of it) partied the previous night like it might have been the last night of their lives.

None reads or dozes. None speaks or checks the view, or fumbles with papers or purse (these are the days before cell phones). All stare forward in a hollowed-out trance.

Our shouting and busy struggles with luggage cease. We gape at a sea of human suffering.

We say nothing, dare not glance at one another. We stand silently. We try to find a respectful place to direct our eyes (out the window, at our shoes) until our stop, heralded by another angry *beeep*, and the doors jerk open. Keeping our eyes lowered— expressing pleasure of any kind would appear obscene—we rush to drag our bags off the car and head out through the cold, still mute with shock, toward the Gare de Lyon.

At first we don't talk about it. Then we say, softly, *Did you see . . . yes . . . my God.*

Now let me cut to a vision from a film we saw, also years ago, called *Lundi Matin* (Monday Morning).

The good and bad part of living in a digital era is that you can look up almost any movie, scan the particulars of its making, read reviews, download it or a trailer for it, and, if you wish, check your memory of it against what you find. Memory often comes up short in these transactions. Yet I sometimes prefer memory, however vague, because that was where the original emotional wallop left its mark. Directed by Otar Ioselliani, the film's lead, a middle-aged character called Vincent, is (movingly) played by Jacques Bidou, a man with a ravaged yet comforting face.

Lundi Matin opens as Vincent wakes to a prototypical day. He lives in a shabby farmhouse somewhere in France with a kvetching, unhappy wife and a couple of bored, indifferent sons. We watch Vincent roll heavily from bed, shuffle around half-conscious shoving dogs and chickens aside, cigarette dangling from his lips. Sitting in his car's driver's seat with his legs hanging out the door, he slips off his beat-up clogs and leaves them where they sit on the grass beside the driveway, donning work boots in the car. He drives to an ugly, toxic chemical factory; smokes a last cigarette furiously before entering. He endures a day of brutal nothingness—forklifts, shrieking machinery, concrete walls—before reversing the procedure at day's end. What floored me—the horribly indelible detail— was when Vincent parks in such a way, once arrived again at home, that he can slip his feet back into those waiting clogs exactly where they sit. No words could make clearer a reality of deadening, infinitely repeated rituals. His wife nags and berates him; his sons ignore him. He paints, sometimes. Life appears loveless and joyless: what the infamous Zorba called "the full catastrophe."

You may think you can guess what follows, but you'll only be partly right. Yes, Vincent leaves one day, wordlessly walks off— with a vague intent to see the world. He goes to Venice. He hangs out with crazy, skanky types; has bizarre misadventures; makes stupid mistakes. In one scene he's thoughtfully watching a puppet show while someone picks his back pocket.

But this picaresque doesn't resolve as one might expect. There's no epiphany, no romantic reunion, no neat tying-off or wised-up aftermath. Vincent eventually returns home, where nothing has changed. A viewer senses that he both is and is not the same. Most of the film runs without dialogue, and most critics found it slow.

It *is* slow. That's part of its payload.

The film showed me things I recognized, things that bear out the findings of other works of art trying to investigate the riddle for which there are many descriptions, and which has been puzzling humankind since we had time and wits to puzzle: awareness of the daily. *Lundi Matin*'s opening uncannily echoes the scene we witnessed in the Paris métro car; both portraits defined by the context of Monday morning. (I would join them, after taking a new job and resuming the act of carting myself to that job every day.)

Director Ioselliani summarized his film thusly: "I made a comedy about the unhappiness of being obligated to obey the rules of this world."

For me there is more to it than that—difficult to convey without sounding glib or psychobabbly. The film's aftermath leaves us altered with a strange understanding, a weird sense of peace and even dignity about the given, about what cannot be recast; something like a better understanding of grief after living with it long enough. If we're lucky (if we get to live long enough), we grasp the quiet reckoning in Vincent's resumption of his life. The unsolved present, the witless density of objects and noise and movement, the zero-sum "this is it-ness" of our days: we may see these conundrums as proof of being alive; also perhaps as a toll of being alive. We may choose to embrace them in the way that Albert Camus implied when he remarked, "One must imagine Sisyphus happy."

Do most of us have to hate our working lives? I don't know. Many, maybe most, appear to feel they have no choice. I remember a lot of clock-watching during day jobs, fervently counting hours and minutes until release—until one day a thoughtful friend reflected that for her, watching the clock on the job was "like selling off little pieces of your body."

For Vincent, something changed, shifting from an abject zombie state (like the young workers in the métro car) to a subtly adjusted awareness. Maybe on the surface that adjustment looks like a form of resignation: survival has always had to be the first task, after all, and resignation (or worse) has certainly been the vision of a boat-load of art. More urgently, the luxury of time, space, and willing-ness to think about what the hell they are doing here (or to look at art suggesting we think about it) may never come for most people. I can't help remembering the father in Robert Hayden's coruscating poem, "Those Winter Sundays." He's nothing like those young French commuters. Yet somehow I see him, and those commuters, and Vincent, and most of the rest of us, connected along a contin-uum. None of these truths cancels out the others. But to me Hayden's father is better than the rest—because he has thought nothing through, and for him whatever day of the week it was could not matter. His is a grace of a heartcutting kind, that perhaps only poetry can explain:

> Sundays too my father got up early
> and put his clothes on in the blueblack cold,
> then with cracked hands that ached
> from labor in the weekday weather made
> banked fires blaze. No one ever thanked him.
> I'd wake and hear the cold splintering, breaking.
> When the rooms were warm, he'd call,
> and slowly I would rise and dress,
> fearing the chronic angers of that house,
> Speaking indifferently to him,
> who had driven out the cold
> and polished my good shoes as well.
> What did I know, what did I know
> of love's austere and lonely offices?

Might the father ever have stopped to see himself, to consider himself performing "love's austere and lonely offices?" Something in us knows he can't.

Coda

I See a Long Journey

I understood everything for a brief period, some while ago.

To the best of my ability to convey this: I really did.

I was driving home, alone, in the morning, after the previous night's reading in another city, at some distance; the drive would take a couple of hours. The reading, my last for this particular book, had gone reasonably well, and I had no immediate, further public presentations to angst about. I felt light and free, relieved to move back into the autonomy, privacy, and comfortable, interior brooding that defines the cycles of my days.

November weather was unstable, dramatic. Cold rain hammered my car like thousands of nails when I set off, soon giving over to great piles of dark, mottled clouds; these moved tensely above the tangled pile of freeway overpasses, the banked, grimy buildings of a passing city. It was a colorless, ugly morning by any definition, but I had good coffee and good music. And now, unbound by formal obligations, I felt a flood of affection to finally see the familiar, low hills hove into view as I neared home; to see cows and fields and splintery old farmhouses in the distance. On the radio, the classics station began to play Rachmaninoff's "Piano Concerto No. 2," and the instant, rich passion of its opening phrases seemed to perfectly describe the movement of weather and earth around me.

Then something happened.

As I gazed at the flow of landscape and traffic, as the music built and swirled and surged—the signal events of my life floated calmly forward and panned across my mind's gaze like some gentle film, for review: I could pick out, at will, any moment, however tiny; any face or setting along the newsreel of my past; I could inhale the very *smells* of the places I'd known. Infancy: staring uncomprehendingly on all fours on the carpet as my kind Uncle Joe, seated across the room, held out his hands to me, coaxing *come on! come on!* Childhood: desert air, cactus blossoms, the chlorinated local swimming pool, the tooth-tugging sweetness of a Snickers bar, the rough, lined paper tablets we learned to write on at grade school, the green lunch ticket that got hole-punched each day, the sterile pungency of the nurse's office. Mother's death. Moving to Sacramento. Teenaged loneliness, bewilderment, listening to the radio late at night as if each song carried a coded message of rescue. Young adulthood: college, West Africa with the Peace Corps, crucial years in a Brigadoon-like Hawaii. Father's death. Migration back to the San Francisco Bay Area; a disastrous love affair. Middle age: graduate school, writing's taking hold.

Good marriage. Friends' deaths. Sister's death. Sister's sons' new babies.

The images moved in measured procession past my mind's eye, a magic lantern.

At the same time, the passage of time itself (as I assume lay minds understand it) became for some reason utterly clear and apprehensible, even *visible*—together with all the generations of human life that had unfolded since we emerged from water, over inconceivable swaths of time.

I swear I am not making this up.

I could see it all—at least, so it felt. I saw time as an endless set of waves, marching in long lines toward shore to break over humans again and again in eternal, stately rhythm: suffering, wild joy, raw birth, wretched death. Wars, terrorism, turmoil. Beauty, mystery, exaltation. I could range backward and forward infinitely over the full panorama—horror to sublimity—without effort, as if my mind's eye were a dial. Whether it was the music, the majestic, roiling weather, the strong, good coffee, or a combination of these, I saw, knew, understood.

It felt bracing, yet calming. Inevitable as air.

Like weather, it was what had been, and what would continue to be. The suffering was inextricable from the joy and boredom and senselessness, and in that blessed interval of clearly grasping this, I felt a deep stillness. The vision conveyed its own perfect, ongoing inevitability. I was able to let go of anguish for my dead—both recent and distant—for the nightmare state of my country and world, for the unanswered valor of human heroism, human stoicism, the excruciating unsolvability of everything. At the same time, I understood quite clearly that I would soon fall back into blinkered, human striving. The shape-shifting clouds, the plaintive imploring of the concerto's piano; its urgent, modern questioning, as if it were pacing a room with accelerating intensity, turning at length to open its arms in exasperated wonder—*now, I ask you!*—and those glowering clouds' haughty answer: *yes, this.* I understood that I will continue to desire, anguish, struggle, imperfectly love those beings in my orbit. I understood, too, more concisely then than ever before, that eventually I will cease, leave those beings and this world. That they will in their turns desire, anguish, struggle to make the best of the time given them and to love the beings in their orbits; sometimes failing, fearing, getting lost or hurt, until they too leave this world and their own beloveds, who will in their turns struggle.

Nothing more, nor less.

Do cats or dogs or birds think such things? Gorillas, dolphins, lizards?

The violins sang *this, this.* The piano rushed and crashed and pooled alongside them.

Filled with a kind of awed attention, accepting for the first time in my life what had always before to me been pretty much unbearable, I wondered whether I might have stumbled upon a state that eastern spiritual disciplines seek. Whatever it was, I felt grateful for even a breath's worth, and hoped I might later be able to remember any of it.

It turns out that I *can* remember it—if not quite to the degree I felt it while driving, underscored by the churning, purling Rachmaninoff. Something about the act of driving that day, the isolation in a moving vehicle, heralded and even *narrated* by the music— entered the bloodstream; became a permanent part of it.

I remember enough, clearly enough, to marvel—and to feel deeply thankful.

I have thought many times about this strange glimpse into the infinite during a simple drive home. A good image for the encounter might be a famous old anonymous woodcut, which first appeared in an 1888 French book about weather. It depicts a humble shepherd (or priest, or preacher) who has managed to wriggle his head and shoulders through the seam at the horizon dividing land from starry heaven. Practically dropping his walking stick in amazement, he beholds the brilliant operating secrets of the universe—the gargantuan, intricate gears and wheels of the cosmos. (Except the awestruck wanderer is not driving a 2008 Toyota Scion.)

Now whenever I happen to catch the strains of the "Concerto No. 2"—and I don't tend to go hunting for it, because who wants to normalize the miraculous, or push their luck—the Cosmic Glimpse (yes, it sounds like a comic book from the sixties) with its overpowering, wheeling-watchworks comprehension, rushes back into my chest: vibrant and mighty yet also, always, strangely soothing. And when I think about it more I consider that a case can be made for time itself as the ultimate place we inhabit, albeit very, very briefly.

When we talk about living somewhere, I have noticed, we generally sound as though we mean, "carrying on this way in perpetuity." Of course that's the dream, the story we tell ourselves. Our lease on inhabitable time is stunningly short. Yet while we are here, in the midst of our little arc, most of us think and act as though it will last forever. (It's mainly older people, I notice, who are able to bring themselves to say, "We will probably live here—this village or town or city, this house, this apartment—until we die.") In fact time is the vastest real estate we know—not that we can genuinely claim to know it, in the intimate, thoroughgoing sense of that word, let alone possess it. We speak of seizing time, seizing the day, but it might be more accurate to say that time is seizing us. Or rather that time coexists with our temporary presence in it, as if we were short-lived guppies in an implacable river. I don't imagine I will ever understand the physics of time, the science of time, of wormholes, spiraling, or (hand over heart for *Wrinkle in Time* author Madeleine L'Engle) tesseracting.

I do know that some comprehensions seem to have to pick their moments to enter us to stay. They have to be spelled into our hand, if you will—in the manner of Helen Keller's suddenly grasping the concept of water, thanks to Annie Sullivan's patient, repeated ministrations. I know now, sharply and viscerally, that what time we have in which to dwell in these humble bodies—thinking, moving, speaking and singing, loving, suffering—is inexpressibly finite. And though most of us are able to sense, on rare and incandescent occasion, that "some things are eternal," we tend to lapse quickly back to grosser, daily concerns. It's too much. Most of us, exempting "saints and poets maybe" (bowing twice to you, Thornton Wilder), aren't built to hold such knowledge at the forefront of thought every minute. Most of us must marshal waking awareness for the survival tasks, marking out our turf. (This, too, soothes us.) To remember now and then that we float, for a flashing moment, in the illimitable space of time, will for most of us be the best we can do. And until the final hour, when (perhaps?) the lens opens all the way before it shuts forever, that will have to be good enough.

Acknowledgments

Warmest thanks to: Centrum Port Townsend, the Ragdale Foundation, and the Vermont Studio Center, where I worked on portions of this collection; my beloved husband Bob Duxbury; distinguished author and poet David Constantine; Nan Cuba, Thaisa Frank, Cornelia Nixon, and Peg Alford Pursell for loving encouragement; Paul Lisicky and Jessie Chaffee for their kind and generous offerings of time and commentary; and friends and family, old and new, near and far, for faith and support.

Passionate thanks to the excellent Joe Mackall, Cassy Brown, and *River Teeth*; to editor Elise McHugh and the University of New Mexico Press, and (in permanent delight) to Phillip Lopate.

Thanks to author David Leavitt for kind permission to quote from his lovely *Florence: A Delicate Case*.

"Those Winter Sundays," © 1966 by Robert Hayden, from *Collected Poems of Robert Hayden* by Robert Hayden, edited by Frederick Glaysher. Used by permission of Liveright Publishing Corporation.

Passage from *The Italians,* © 1964 by Luigi Barzini, used by permission of Simon & Schuster.

Finally, I thank the editors of the below publications, where many of these pieces, in slightly different form, first appeared:

Rosebud: "The Where of It"
The Antioch Review: "Cake Frosting Country"
The Antioch Review: "The Astonishment Index"

TriQuarterly Online: "In Case of Firenze"

Woven Tale Press: "Shake Me Up, Judy"

Stoneboat *(now dedicated to Rebecca Winterer's Florentine bag):* "A Bag of One's Own"

The Writing Disorder: "Little Traffic Light Men"

River Teeth: "Cave of the Iron Door"

Wilderness House Literary Review: "Red State, Blue State: A Short, Biased Lament"

WomenArts Quarterly: "Today I Will Fly"

Another Chicago Magazine: "Place as Answer: HGTV"

Lowestoft Chronicle: "Location Sluts"

The Culture-ist: "Rules for the Well-Intended"

Chicago Review Quarterly: "I See a Long Journey: Time as Place" [Coda]